## Also by Carole Marsh Longmeyer

### SLIGHTLY SOUTH OF HEAVEN
Sensational and Unsavory Crimes in the Lowcountry

### DEATH BY GRITS
Surprising Tales of Murder by Food, Often at the Hands of Your Favorite Person

### THE KUDZU COOKBOOK
Cooking Up a Storm with That Wild & Crazy Vine That Grows in Miles-Per-Hour!

### LOWCOUNTRY VOODOO A to Z
The Real Lowdown on Historical Gullah Voodoo, Past and Present!

# LOWCOUNTRY HURRICANES

## A to Z

-INCLUDING MATTHEW 2016-

**CAROLE MARSH LONGMEYER**

Author of Lowcountry Voodoo A to Z

GALLOPADE

Copyright 2016 Carole Marsh Longmeyer
All rights reserved.

Printed in the United States of America.

Published by Gallopade International,
Peachtree City, Georgia.

For permissions or author interview, contact Gallopade at
800-536-2438.

Lowcountry Hurricanes Team:

Susan Van Denhende, Graphic Design
Jon McKenna, Gallopade New Product Development
Janice Baker, Editor
John Hanson, Art Director
Tommy Dean, Printing and Binding

This book is dedicated to the caregivers, aides, nurses, and others who help evacuate patients from hospitals, nursing homes, and other facilities when there is a hurricane evacuation. They bring the meds, the pets, and all the patients need. They do this under great duress, especially since they often leave their own families to do their jobs. In some circumstances (*Katrina*/New Orleans, for example), they may be stranded in hospitals with patients, perhaps with water flooding in, in darkness, in fear, and do whatever is essential to keep patients alive. That they prepare, implement, and recover from such disasters and often get little notice or recognition makes me appreciate them even more.

# Table of Contents

Introduction ............................................. 11
Note on References ............................... 15
Foreword................................................ 17
A to Z ..................................................... 24
Bibliography ......................................... 168
Hurricane Quotations .......................... 173

# LOWCOUNTRY HURRICANES A TO Z

CAROLE MARSH LONGMEYER
DESIGNED BY SUSAN VAN DENHENDE

## Gone With the Wind...

I have lived in hurricane country most of my life. It's exciting, all right, but dangerous as well. At least we have a warning (most of the time, these days), unlike long ago when folks depended on a glint of green in the sky or an ache in their get-a-long. But the luxury of warnings is useless if you don't heed a mandatory evacuation order. Oh, now you know that, *Matthew* survivors?

My first hurricane was quite a bit inland, in Bath, oldest town in North Carolina and Golden Age of Piracy haunt of Blackbeard and crew. It seemed safe to stay in our eighteen-inch thick walled home. However, when Mother Nature snaked up the Pamlico River into Bath Creek right to our front door, I knew we'd sorely miscalculated. Husband Bob held the French doors closed with his belt, while I "sot" (to use an old-timey Elizabethan term) on the sandbags at the front door to keep them from floating away. We ventured out when the eye passed over to spy an orb of serene sky speckled with stars. Within the span of a breath, the second string of the hurricane hit and we dashed into the house and back into our hold-the-fort positions. It was a long night.

While living on idyllic Emerald Isle at the south end of the Outer Banks, we hauled personal belongings and home office equipment down four flights of stairs to evacuate to New Bern before Hurricane *Bertha's* big, fat fanny clobbered the shore. We were far enough inland to allow us to enjoy a safe hurricane party at an inn populated by many of our neighbors. We did not question our hurried escape when we returned to find that prison chain gangs from Raleigh were walking the beachfront shoulder-to-shoulder to pick up the gazillion pieces of shingles and such. The beautiful, mature and well-vegetated dunes that God had put there once upon a time had been scrubbed flat, the sand shoved to fill all the pools to the brim.

Forty-five days later, while we were enjoying a vacation in the Northwoods of Minnesota, *Fran* barreled down the exact same path—through Camp Lejeune and across Emerald Isle. Disgusted, our neighbor stayed put during the storm. When I called to check on them, she managed to share (just before the phone service vanished) that in her oceanfront kitchen "the tiles on the floor are dancing!" We hastily returned to find an eerie fairyland, where all the newly plunked down dunes (aka a pile of loose sand) had been blasted onto every surface, every structure sparkling in the sun. This time, no one came. We sold our place and moved to a house, rented sight-unseen, in Colorado Springs, Colorado.

You do know that most bridges are closed when the wind is a mere 45 miles per hour, don't you? And if you choose to stay, no one can stop you. At Emerald Isle, the authorities, canvassing door-to-door, only ask one question, "Who is your next of kin?"

But it's not the wind or the rain that scares me. I do love a big ol' blowin' storm. It's the history. If *Hugo* and *Katrina* are not enough to scare the boogie board shorts off of you, then read about Galveston, or *Floyd*, that bamboozled its way so far inland that it stripped apples off the trees in the orchards in the mountains of North Carolina. Read about McClellanville, South Carolina, where daddies had to shove their kids in the rafters of an open shelter, then cling themselves, mouths tightly closed, to tenuous handholds until the storm surge abated.

In Bath, an older man once told me the tale of a potato boat caught in a storm. A bride and her bridesmaids were aboard, along with a passel of spuds headed to market. When the wind capsized the boat, the brave black captain (who could not swim) tried to save the girls. All were lost. The same winds blew blue crabs out of the creek and into the white picket-fenced yards on the shore. It was then I knew I was fascinated by hurricanes and would write about them some day.

Carole Marsh Longmeyer
Wilson Village, elevation 20 feet
Palmetto Bluff
Bluffton, South Carolina

PS: We don't call it the Lowcountry for nothin'; evacuate. If a hurricane is anything, it's where you don't want to find yourself at the wrong place at the wrong time. I know.

# Notes on References

I often find that after I write a book, folks ask me where I got such great information. My special references for this book include:

**LOWCOUNTRY HURRICANES**
**Three Centuries of Storms at Sea and Ashore**
Walter J. Fraser Jr.
The University of Georgia Press

**South Carolina, A History**
Walter B. Edgar
University of South Carolina Press

**North Carolina's Hurricane History**
Jay Barnes
The University of North Carolina Press

And regarding Hurricane *Matthew*, the great work by *The Island Packet*, *The Bluffton News*, *The Savannah Morning News*, and other Lowcountry media.

# Matthew

The instigation for writing this book at this time was *Matthew*—the hurricane that was not supposed to come our way. At least that's what everyone had said for years—a couple of hundred, to be exact. "We can't get hit by a hurricane," was the standard mantra. "We're in the Georgia Bight; we're protected." But those who knew the history, knew differently.

Nonetheless, each year we'd watch the seasonal parade of tropical storms form out in the Atlantic and commiserate when they pummeled the Caribbean or the Keys, engorge the Gulf or march on over to Mexico.

Yes, of course, some would beat a path to Bermuda, slam dunk Cape Hatteras and the Outer Banks, or even as a tropical storm or "near miss," bluster around over Georgia and the Carolinas. Our hearts broke over *Hugo* and *Katrina*. But since the 1800s, we'd not had a direct hit and grew complacent. In the twelve years I lived in the Historic District of Savannah, I'd never seen those "contra-flow" traffic gates closed on Interstate 16.

The truth is that *Matthew* was not a "direct hit" either, but the vehemence of an eye wall a mere ten miles from shore and a mandatory evacuation that took many by surprise, as well as the resulting damage from Savannah to Charleston, especially in Beaufort, Bluffton, Hilton Head Island, Daufuskie Island, Edisto, and on up into the Carolinas, certainly counted as a hurricane from hell.

# Major Lowcountry Hurricanes

Early Unnamed Hurricanes (offshore storms not listed)

| | |
|---|---|
| 1686 | Charleston, SC |
| 1700 | Charleston, SC |
| 1713 | Charleston, SC |
| 1724 | Lowcountry |
| 1728 | Charleston, SC |
| 1743 | SC coast |
| 1747 | SC coast |
| 1752 | "The Great Hurricane," Charleston (Sept. 13-15) |
| 1752 | SC coast (Sept. 30-Oct. 1) |
| 1758 | GA and SC coast |
| 1769 | GA and SC coast |
| 1770 | GA and SC coast |
| 1778 | GA and SC coast |
| 1781 | SC coast |
| 1783 | GA and SC coast |
| 1797 | Charleston, SC |
| 1804 | Georgia and SC coast |
| 1813 | Lower Georgia coast |
| 1820 | Georgetown, SC |

| | |
|---|---|
| 1822 | Upper SC coast |
| 1824 | SC coast; St. Simons/Darien, GA |
| 1830 | Upper SC coast |
| 1834 | Georgetown, SC |
| 1835 | GA and SC |
| 1837 | Lower GA coast |
| 1842 | Lower GA coast |
| 1846 | Lowcountry |
| 1848 | GA coast |
| 1851 | GA coast |
| 1853 | GA and SC coast |
| 1854 | Brunswick and Savannah, GA |
| 1871 | St. Simons, GA |
| 1874 | Lowcountry |
| 1878 | South Charleston, SC |
| 1881 | GA and SC coast |
| 1885 | GA and SC coast |
| 1893 | Tybee Island, GA |
| 1893 | Georgetown, SC |
| 1896 | GA and SC coast |
| 1898 | GA and SC coast |
| 1898 | Cumberland Island, GA |
| 1904 | Upper SC coast |
| 1906 | Upper SC coast |
| 1911 | Savannah, GA |
| 1916 | Upper SC coast |

1928    St. Marys, GA
1940    Beaufort/Edisto, SC
1947    GA coast

Named Hurricanes:

1952    *Able* Edisto, SC
1954    *Hazel* SC/NC border
1959    *Gracie* Beaufort, SC
1964    *Dora* Lower GA coast
1979    *David* Ossabaw Island, Tybee Island, Savannah
1989    *Hugo* Upper SC coast
1999    *Floyd* Offshore SC/NC coast
2004    *Alex* NC/GA
2004    *Charley* Myrtle Beach, SC
2004    *Gaston* Lowcountry
2014    *Arthur* NC
2016    *Matthew* FL, GA, SC, NC

**AARON BURR:** You can run, but you can't hide, from a hurricane. On Tuesday, September 4, 1804, Aaron Burr, vice president of the United States, was at Hampton Plantation on St. Simon's Island, Georgia, hiding out from federal authorities for the murder (in a duel, as you know) of Treasury Secretary Alexander Hamilton. The island proved to be in the direct line of a massive hurricane. Burr had rowed to a nearby plantation and found he was unable to cross the water back to Hampton. That night, the hurricane made landfall. Burr was witness to all that such a high-powered storm can do. As the eye passed over, he made a run back to Hampton Plantation where he rode out the rest of the storm.

**ABLE:** The U.S. Weather Bureau named this August 1952 storm *Able*. (This was a year before they switched to giving hurricanes women's names.) Edisto Island took the brunt of this storm, getting clobbered by the dreaded right front quadrant. It also came ashore after dark, always a fearful time for those hunkered down but unable to see what the wind and water are doing. Extensive damage at Edisto included pre-fab "hutments" being used as beach cottages. At Hardeeville the rains were so harsh and visibility so limited, plus winds so high, that automobiles were lifted from the road and spun around. One such accident killed two people. Fortunately, U.S. Navy ships were moved up the river or sent to sea, due to advance warnings that allowed enough time to do so. South Carolina was lucky this time.

**ACT OF CONGRESS:** In 1870, the U.S. Congress passed an act creating the United States Weather Bureau. This law required the Signal Corps to warn of the "approach and force of storms...on the seacoast by magnetic telegraph and marine signals." The act also created a network of observers along the Atlantic and Gulf coasts.

Weather bureaus were later established at Savannah and Charleston, at last leading to more advance warning of hurricanes.

**AFRICA:** On September 13, 1752, the slave ship *Africa* found itself in the middle of a hurricane offshore of Savannah. Captain John Dorrington attempted to steer into the engorged sea. As he lost headway, his ship's sails, rigging and masts were drenched and destroyed. Incredibly, the *Africa* remained afloat, though foundering, in the enormous waves. With no way to control the ship, it was blown northward to Charles Town and beyond. Eventually pounding against the sandbars of the North Edisto River, the ship was abandoned. While some of the crew and slaves were blown overboard to their deaths, those remaining were rescued and saved.

**AFRICAN AMERICANS:** Historically, some of the hardest-hit residents of the Lowcountry during hurricanes are black residents living in low-lying coastal areas. Slaves in early America generally could not swim and often lost their lives in the storm surge. If they evacuated via ship with their masters, they sometimes drowned when the vessels foundered and sank beneath the waves or were pounded to smithereens on sandbars. Often, as heroes, they gave their lives to save others. Fishermen of the "Mosquito Fleet" in Charleston often fell afoul of deadly weather during unnamed, unannounced hurricanes. Even today, coastal African American communities face great risks from rising water and high winds and trade generally serene surroundings for treachery during hurricanes.

**ALEX:** This August 2004 hurricane brushed the Outer Banks of North Carolina. It produced strong waves and moderate flooding. One person drowned in the surf. Hundreds of vehicles and homes were flooded.

**AMERICAN REVOLUTION HURRICANE OF 1778:** Obviously, this was two years after 1776, a high tide mark of prosperity for the Carolina colonies. At Charles Town, South Carolina, the war, a fire that burned more than 250 structures and the beginning of a powerful string of hurricanes threw commercial and agricultural progress into a tailspin. In August 1778, an unnamed hurricane not only came ashore at Georgetown, South Carolina, it spread all the way up to New Bern, North Carolina. Ships and the coast were badly beaten down, but the unrelenting torrents of rain and the howling wind also headed inland to destroy trees, crops and buildings in the central and even western part of the colony. For years, the British and the French lost ships in hurricanes. Indeed, 1780 proved to be one of the deadliest hurricane seasons—numerous storms killed thousands from the Caribbean and all up the coast of Florida, Georgia, the Carolinas to Cape Hatteras and beyond to Rhode Island. Great deluge followed by severe drought brought further hurricanes ashore. So battered was their fleet, that by 1782, the British withdrew their troops from the Lowcountry.

**ANY PORT IN A STORM?:** One thing hurricanes prove is that you can hunker down in as sturdy a structure as available and yet still be killed by rising water or a collapsed chimney. As well, you can cling precariously to something as flimsy as a floating hen coop, as one man did for 24 hours, until he was saved. Another unusual bolt-hole was the local lazaretto, or quarantine station, such as the one located on Tybee Island, Georgia, during the slave trade era.

**"A PERFECTLY WHITE MOUNTAINOUS SEA":** That's how one person described the 1854 major hurricane that took aim on the southeastern U.S. coast. Ships, including the *Star of the South*, *Angenett*, *Edward Kidder*, *Mary Ann* and *Dirigo*, duked it out with the storm, winning some rounds, losing others. On the South Carolina coast, the *Delia Maria* was soon dismasted. Passengers and crew reached safety on Hilton Head via small boats. A ship was found bottom-up off Dewees Island. The *Les Amis Reunis*, a French schooner, "went to pieces" at Lavender Point on Bull's Island. Close by, the *Caroline Hall* was blown into the marsh. The *Jane* was dismasted and floated away to sea. The

*Margaret Davis*, trying to assist the *E. Hinds*, ended up plowing into the ship. Captains in the seas from Charleston to Savannah were appalled at the number of battered ships floating freely in the water, with no answer to come when they tried to hail them. One captain swore he sailed through "the heaviest sea ever experienced during the 25 years…at sea." Retreat Plantation did not feel like much of one to Anna King, who had been running the plantation alone in her husband's absence. "The wind is so high & so jerks this house I find it hard to write," she noted. "Look for trouble this night," warned Hugh Grant from Elizafield Plantation. One planter worried that the full moon and high tides would create a perfect storm of devastation of his 3,700 acres of crop fields.

**ARTHUR:** It hit eastern North Carolina with 100 mile-per-hour winds on July 3 and 4, 2014.

**ATLANTIC BASIN:** Basically, the Atlantic Ocean, from which tropical storms may form, travel and make landfall.

**ATLANTIC EMBAYMENT:** Another name for the Georgia Bight. This part of the Lowcountry extends approximately ten miles inland from the sea from Myrtle Beach, South Carolina, to St. Marys, Georgia, or in a larger sense, from the Outer Banks of North Carolina to Cape Canaveral, Florida.

**AUGUST 18-19, 1871:** This was one of the first hurricanes where those onshore and at sea had some advance warning via "weather reports." Nonetheless, in the Lowcountry, the unbelievable battering of everything not nailed down continued unabated. A 1,230-ton steamship, the *Liberty*, barely limped into Tybee Island after its rudder was smashed and it became unnavigable. A load of railroad iron ended up on the sea bottom after the *Sabino* sunk, though all hands were rescued. You could sail a boat down Broughton Street in Savannah, the water was so high. Three ships loading phosphate at Beaufort, South Carolina, were driven ashore. In Charleston, wind and rain carved holes in the street large enough to hold "a carriage and horse."

**BATHHOUSE BLUES:** The 1874 hurricane forced the family of Michael McMamnon into a tiny beachside bathhouse after a bridge went out and left them stranded on the shore. An audience of onlookers gathered on the Battery in Charleston to watch and worry over the father, mother, two children and a friend as they huddled inside the flimsy structure being battered left and right in the winds. First, some fishermen tried to rescue the family; next, the police; then, the Palmetto Boat crew, but their craft capsized. After some of these would-be rescuers had to be rescued, a man tied a rope to his waist and swam out to the boathouse where he managed to rescue one of the small children. At last, the eye of the storm passed over, giving others a chance to rescue the rest of the family. When the winds returned, the bathhouse sank beneath the waves almost immediately.

**BEACHFRONT MANAGEMENT ACT:** Enacted by the South Carolina General Assembly, this law attempted to curb irresponsible building in already vulnerable low-lying coastal areas, especially anything that impeded the protection and growth of naturally-occurring and well-vegetated sand dunes. Nonetheless, construction to the contrary continued, and continues today.

**BEAUFORT, SOUTH CAROLINA:** In 1804, a hurricane destroyed a causeway that had been under construction for the previous seven years "at great expense." A high storm surge also flooded and ruined a number of other bridges, so that any travel between the islands in the area was completely impossible. So massive was the flooding, that rice fields were inundated and destroyed and so many animals drowned that the stench was unbearable.

**BERTHA:** Life in hurricane country is always interesting. When hurricane *Bertha* came ashore on the lower end of the Outer Banks of North Carolina, between Camp Lejeune and

Morehead City, dangerous rip currents kept lifeguards busy and led to many rescues. The date was July 12, 1996. Just 45 days later, *Fran* slammed into the same area. We lived at Emerald Isle, accessible only via bridges over a sound. While we evacuated, neighbors who stayed in their oceanfront home called to tell us that "the tiles on the kitchen floor are dancing up and down!"

**BIG HURRICANE, 1911:** It's amazing how many weather reports on the day of a storm read something like, "Light winds, fair weather." However, later the same day on August 27, 1911, the National Weather Bureau issued a sudden warning for an imminent hurricane. Such a late warning was a death knell for ships already out to sea in the face of the storm. Ship captains off the Carolina coast estimated winds up to 100 miles per hour. So horrendous was the damage that marine officials reported, "It will be a long time before all of the wrecks are discovered and the loss of life at sea is figured up." To this day, there is no final reckoning. The hurricane finally came ashore at Savannah. In addition to other destruction, two windmills that provided Tybee Island with fresh water were blown over. The marsh was littered with craft blown up the creeks. In the city, residents had to cope with new problems, such as the loss of telephone and telegraph wires, and the loss of power when electric lines were ripped loose. Thirty-six hours of high winds just about swept away Beaufort, South Carolina. With a population of 7,000 blacks on St. Helena Island, the resulting destruction was said to have ended with everything from "great discomfort" to "a year of famine, want and suffering… Fever and sickness adds to the distress…" Crops were ruined from Savannah to Charleston. In Charleston, the storm tore flagstones from the Battery and 100-pound cannon balls tumbled like tennis balls. The storm surge flooded the streets and buildings with 11 feet of water. Winds were said to be in excess of 100 miles per hour, but the actual velocity is unknown since the weather bureau's wind gauge blew away! A drawbridge was said to have spun around like the arrow on a child's board game. Collapsing buildings killed many: the Wapoo Mill, the Mt. Pleasant town hall, the Consolidated Railway's ticket office, and many others. At Fort Moultrie on Sullivan's Island, soldiers formed hand-to-hand lifelines to haul people out of deep water to safety. Sharks and porpoises came ashore and were washed far inland by the rising waters. The Carolina Gold rice culture came to an end, devastating Lowcountry economies. Alas, the cotton, lumber and naval stores industries also admitted defeat. It was said that following this fateful storm, the Lowcountry was likely "the poorest part of the poorest census region in the United States."

**BILL:** This Category Four hurricane churned up the Atlantic Ocean off the coast of the Carolinas in August 2009. Rough surf and powerful rip currents created the need for many water rescues.

**BLOW OF 1728:** The people of Charles Towne were always nervous when the weather became "uncommonly hot." The heat had already wreaked havoc with ruined crops, dead cattle, an epidemic of yellow fever, and near starvation. When the hurricane blew ashore in the night, many residents fled to the roofs of their houses in an attempt to get above the rapidly rising storm surge; many died. Twenty-three ships were destroyed and more than 2,000 barrels of rice were washed away. Thousands of trees were blown down in the city as well as inland.

**BLUFFTON, SOUTH CAROLINA:** Although Bluffton is on a bluff on the May River, which puts it about twenty feet above the water, hurricanes like *Hugo* still managed to sock a mighty punch with waves ocean-height. During *Matthew*, Old Town, an active area in the process of major growth, endured plenty of wind and water. Adjacent Highway 46, the May River Road, lost many old oak trees. I live in Bluffton, in Palmetto Bluff, at about twenty feet above sea level, but those towering pines from this old Union Camp property took baseball-like bats at many homes. This storm was not bluffing, but every inch above the water table is an inch closer to staying high and dry.

**BOB:** The first hurricane of the 1985 season, *Bob* made landfall near Beaufort, South Carolina, on July 25. Although the storm weakened over land, it still caused $20 million in damages and five indirect deaths.

**BONNIE:** While the eye of this hurricane in August 1998 did not hit South Carolina, it did $30 million in damage just across the border in North Carolina, where it made landfall near Wilmington.

**CAPE ROMAIN AND RACCOON KEYS:** This outcropping and barrier islands off the Lowcountry of South Carolina are sort of our version of Cape Hatteras, meaning they can't catch a break in a hurricane. Already littered with an incessant flow of shipwrecks, this Mother Lode of debris was added to in 1815 when the *Spring*, a 140-ton British brig was snagged after midnight on August 31. Sparing nothing but the crew and "the clothes they were wearing," the ship and its cargo were lost on the hurricane-washed shoals. The storm moseyed on to slam the coast all the way up to eastern North Carolina, leaving a stream of bodies and sunken ships in its wake.

**CAROLINA GOLD:** One of the main export crops at risk during hurricane season was the wealth-maker—Carolina Gold rice.

Often striking when the crops were near peak production, the ruin of thousands of acres was financially devastating. The occasional lull in hurricanes over a period of years just meant a larger crop of "gold" to destroy when the next "big one" came along. Today, a limited amount of this delicious rice is still grown in the Lowcountry.

**CATASTROPHIC HURRICANE, GA, 1824:** It was yet another September storm. Ships at sea—a fleet of nine British vessels, the *Albion*, the *John and Mary*, the *Martha Forbes*, the *West Indian*, the *Wilding*, the pilot boat *Friends*—were lost at sea or smashed upon sandbars. Next, the storm stalked the schooner *Jane*, the brig *Caroline Ann*, the *Maria*, *Emperor*, *Vexation*, *Governor Hopkins*, the *Hunter* and more. The death toll rose. But the powerhouse hurricane still had plenty left when it came ashore. St. Simons, Darien, Cumberland Island, Jekyll, Sapelo, Cockspur, Edisto, Folly, and all along the most low-lying of the Lowcountry were severely affected. One hundred sheep drowned on Little St. Simons Island. Giant live oaks were uprooted and tossed about. Cotton crops worth millions were destroyed. At least 83 people drowned on St. Simons Island alone. Structures that had survived previous hurricanes blew away: a hospital, storehouse, carriage house, lightkeeper's house, sugar mill, and more. Many slaves saved themselves when their cabins washed away only by climbing into trees. The emotional toll was incalculable, especially when you hear of children being snatched by the wind right out of a parent's arms. As one person concluded about this hurricane of horror: "Nothing appears around us here but a scene of destruction."

**CATASTROPHIC HURRICANE, SC, 1822:** This vicious storm occurred on September 27-28. Like most massive hurricanes, you can predict and imagine the depth and breadth of devastation. But perhaps this storm was defined by the many and varied types of deaths. Sailors, of course, were blown overboard and drowned. One boy drowned in the cabin of a sloop washed into the marsh. Some men and women drowned trying to get ashore ahead of their foundered vessel.

Ashore, collapsing houses crushed women, children, servants and slaves. A large beam crushed one woman, while another made her way to the beach, where she was blown into high water and drowned. A slave girl died on the threshold of the house she was trying to escape from. Some died inside from collapsed chimneys, while others died when they fled outdoors. At Pinckney Horry Plantation, 50 of 55 slaves drowned. A woman was swept out to sea, drowned, and then returned to the beach. Another woman was crushed and drowned in her bed; a slave and her child, who slept beneath the bed, also died. When the home of Dr. Levi Myers was swept into the sea, he and 14 members of his family perished. One family took refuge in an outhouse and managed to survive. Because the hurricane struck so suddenly and with so little warning, people were caught off guard. The death toll was never known, especially since others died in creeks and waterways deep into the wetlands of the Lowcountry. While a death toll in the hundreds was estimated originally, later, many believed the true toll was in the thousands.

**CENTRAL AMERICA:** Not all Lowcountry hurricanes battered the shores. An 1857 storm stayed offshore, where it pummeled more than 50 vessels stranded at sea. The *Central America*, returning from the gold fields with 572 crew and passengers, plus $27+ million in gold aboard, was blindsided by the hurricane. This was an extremely sturdy three-masted steamer and side-wheeler. Even at 280 feet in length with a 40-foot beam, it was no match for Mother Nature. From a gentle breeze and pleasant whitecaps, the weather deteriorated to 60-knot winds and sideways rain squalls. Giant waves washed over the bow and into cabins. Leaks, then rising water, put out the fires in the boilers. Pumps and engines shut down and the captain resorted to sails, which immediately blew away. A desperate bucket brigade proved to be a worthless task. Water assaulted the ship in "an avalanche" "mountains high." The crew hastily built rafts from any furniture, boards, even pieces of ship itself, in anticipation of a necessary abandonment. Another storm-battered ship, the *Marine*, appeared and was able to take aboard all the women and children. The remaining passengers and crew were issued life preservers. As many as possible were ferried to the *Marine*. However, after dark, the *Central America* went down stern first, spilling some people overboard—some were thrown clear and grabbed anything that floated and were saved. The remaining poor souls were sucked beneath the sea with the ship. The captain and first mate went down with the ship, still at their posts. At least 423 people perished; a few survivors were rescued in the next few hours and days. At that time, this event was the single greatest maritime disaster involving a U.S. commercial vessel and a hurricane.

**CHARLESTON, SOUTH CAROLINA:** This gorgeous city proved ground zero for horrendous hurricane *Hugo*. Used to tropical storms, marauding pirates and frequent hurricanes, no one expected the massive devastation and loss of life this storm wrought.

**CHARLEY:** This mid-August 2004 storm struck Florida's west coast with 145 mile-per-hour winds. Then it moved east across the state and left destruction in its wake as it left Jacksonville and headed north. A mandatory evacuation was called for South Carolina. Charleston was spared much damage since winds were light. It was worse at Georgetown, and then Myrtle Beach's Grand Strand took the brunt of the storm. Caught between two weather systems, *Charley* moved back offshore. But another hurricane was on the way—*Gaston*!

**CINDY:** The leftover winds and water of this 2005 hurricane spawned eight tornadoes in North Carolina.

**CIVIL WAR:** Even the maelstrom of the Civil War could not interrupt the spawning of hurricanes and their eventual trek to the Lowcountry. In 1862, just a year after the firing on Fort Sumter, yet another hurricane attacked the Lowcountry. It was the start of another cycle of storms destined to blow our way. In October 1865, a 56-hour "gale" took down a warship filled with gold. Forty-two passengers and crew survived; 17 did not.

The *Republic's* location was recently found, and its gold and silver coins are estimated to be worth $180 million today.

### COASTAL HURRICANE OF 1722:

During this violent Lowcountry storm, the wind and water were so strong and high that it was noted "deer were frequently found lodged in tall trees." Inland, panthers and bears suffered the same fate.

### COCKSPUR ISLAND:

Site of the sweet little Cockspur Light, in one unnamed early hurricane, residents fled to nearby Fort Pulaski for safety; every house except for one was swept into the Savannah River.

### CONSTRUCTION FOR DESTRUCTION:

People have always pondered and explored ways to build "hurricane-proof" homes. Thomas Spalding, a trader, planter and student of weather, decided to construct a home to withstand the violent hurricanes bound to attack his Lowcountry home on Atlantic Ocean-facing Sapelo Island, Georgia.

It took three years to build South End House, which was built quite low to the ground with three-foot-thick walls made of tabby, recessed columns and square-hewn timbers.

*This is why you evacuate!*

**COTTON AND OTHER CROPS:** While we think of hurricanes destroying homes and businesses and downing trees, the destruction of crops such as cotton, rice, indigo, and even during Matthew, massive groves of nut-filled pecan trees—just to give a few examples—can ruin not only the products ready for market, but the future of struggling farmers for seasons to come.

**CYCLES OF HURRICANES:** If you research the many hurricane seasons recorded, you begin to see a pattern of cycles of lots of hurricanes, more or less alternating with fewer such storms. Nonetheless, nothing seems to prevent a "big one" in an off season, or a hurricane during the so-called "non-hurricane season." Mother Nature is always full of surprises. A number of seasons with no or few hurricanes striking an area seems to bring a kind of unwise complacency. I have read that the 1990s began a new cycle of hurricanes that may last 30 to 40 years! From 1995-1999, Atlantic hurricanes occurred more frequently than in any prior five-year period. No less than five Category Four hurricanes occurred in 1999 alone, something never witnessed in hurricane data collection history. It often seems to be feast or famine for the Lowcountry. So was *Matthew* 2016 an exception, or a new rule? Only time, and tide, will tell. And what of global warming and rising sea levels? So far, nothing seems to be bad enough to scare folks away from the lovely place we call the Lowcountry. But if a hurricane comes along named Voodoo, I'm outta here!

**DAUFUSKIE ISLAND, SC:** This lovely barrier island made famous by beloved Lowcountry author Pat Conroy, lives up to his memoir *The Water is Wide* during hurricanes, when the water is also high. Accessible only by boat or ferry, die-hards remained behind during *Matthew*. A 2,000+ guest music event had to be canceled due to the mandatory evacuation. Power was not restored for a month after the hurricane passed.

**DAVID:** This 1979 hurricane was among the first to be given a male name. It had been awhile since a hurricane had hit the Lowcountry. Indeed the 1970s had seen the lowest number of storms to come ashore in the U.S. *David* seemed a demon as it hit the West Indies with winds over 140 miles per hour, killing more than 2,000 people. In spite of being called a "monster storm," *David* hit Palm Beach, Florida, with just 85 mile-per-hour winds. However, the storm then headed out over the Atlantic Ocean, picked up strength, and now referred to as a "killer storm," bore down on Tybee Island, Georgia. By the time the hurricane came ashore, many—but not all—people had evacuated. The Lowcountry got lucky. The storm did the usual damage to local structures, including the Bethesda Home for Boys in Savannah, the Georgia Ports Authority, and the Savannah Ice Delivery Company. Due to a lack of generators, radio and television stations went off the air. At Daufuskie Island, Hilton Head, Beaufort, Folly Beach, and Charleston, damage was also relatively light. Of course, not so much at Litchfield Beach, where 13 homes were destroyed. People found the Red Cross, other agencies, and the civil defense system quite helpful before and after the storm. This was not "the big one," but had this Category Five hurricane not been somewhat shredded when it swept over Haiti's mountains before coming ashore in the Lowcountry as a Category Two, things might have been quite different.

**DAY THAT WAS DIFFERENT:** By 1898, weather warnings were more established, so that instead of being totally blindsided by an unsuspected hurricane, people now lived in fear and dread of announced impending storms. While there were no formal evacuations, people at least could prepare, and vacationers in the Lowcountry often returned to their homes a bit earlier than planned. A "warning" could be as little as, in the instance of this storm, four hours ahead, and not quite on the mark, as this one was assumed to be a mere tropical storm. However, when this hurricane blasted ashore at Tybee Island, Georgia, it was packing 100-mile-per-hour winds, which blew away the tents of the army unit stationed there. A windmill and a water tower collapsed, and the usual damage was done to homes and shops. Next, the storm hauled itself over Wassau and Wilmington Islands, and Thunderbolt. Eight inches of rain fell in Savannah, a record. Again, the usual damage was done to homes, churches, theaters, and stores—but this time looting occurred in the shops. Alas, on Hilton Head, white residents who collected food and supplies for affected

African Americans were attacked by some of these men, and the goods were taken by force.

**DONNA:** In 1960, this storm hit Florida and then scooted on up the Lowcountry coast as a Category Two storm. In eastern North Carolina, it did a lot of damage near Wilmington, Nags Head and Topsail Beach.

**DORA:** This *Dora* was an explorer, looking for the Lowcountry, and finding it, in September 1964. First striking at St. Augustine, Florida, this "well-organized and dangerous" hurricane's 125 mile-per-hour winds caused the cancellation of a Beatles' concert. By the time the storm reached the Georgia coast, you did need a yellow submarine to cope with the 13-foot tidal surge, enormous rains and gigantic waves. This was the most powerful storm to hit Georgia since 1898. *Dora's* right front quadrant fist pounded the shore for 18 straight hours. Numerous drownings occurred, as did lots of standard damage to trees, homes, power lines and poles, and the beach itself. The beautiful King and Prince Hotel at

St. Simons was barely saved from flooding by the use of hastily built dikes. "It's worse than you told me," was President Lyndon Johnson's comment after visiting post-storm. Fortunately, television reports and more advance and accurate weather warnings saved lives by encouraging citizens in the most low-lying areas to evacuate. The overall estimate of damage was valued at $280 million.

**EARL:** This 2010 storm passed just east of North Carolina's Outer Banks. More than $2.5 million in damages was reported, including the washout of Highway 12 on the coast and crop damage inland. An earlier *Earl* in 1998 was less severe, although it did create a minor tornado outbreak throughout parts of the Lowcountry, resulting in three deaths.

**EARLY SEASON HURRICANE, 1825:** It started slamming the Florida coast on June 3, quite early in the hurricane season. The captain of the schooner *Magnolio* said he saw large seabirds, unable to use their wings, blown through the air for long distances and dropped into the sea. At Tybee Island, Georgia, the pilot boat *Georgia Ann* was washed up onto Potato Point, near Cockspur Island. After charging on up through the

Carolina coast, the stubborn storm continued on to New England.

**END OF A CYCLE:** It is true that hurricane activity can come in cycles. From the 1800s to the early 1900s, a steady stream of hurricanes battered the Lowcountry. This ended (for a while) in 1916, which was a very active hurricane season—with eleven storms! Fortunately, there was adequate warning of the July storm. That was a good thing since it was the height of vacation season. People hurried onto ferries to get off the resort sea islands before the storm struck. Being out and about was foolish: one man was electrocuted by a live wire, and another washed over the edge of his sloop and drowned. Off Charleston, ships foundered left and right. One of them was a coal barge; the captain and crew drowned. At McClellanville, boats were perched in the streets and dead chickens, raccoons, and seabirds found in the water. For 22 miles, from the Awendaw Bridge to the Santee River, 90 out of every 100 pines were downed. On Pawley's Island, a man ran door to door to warn of the storm; residents and vacationers dashed over the causeway in 100-mile-per-hour winds. The next hurricane would not arrive until 1928.

**END-OF-THE-CENTURY:** Near the end of the 1800s, a string of hurricanes belted the Lowcountry. A September 1878 storm was especially rough from Georgia to Cape Hatteras, North Carolina. Hitting the South Carolina coast at high tide, the storm surge not only ruined rice fields near harvest, it washed stores of rice out to sea, and pretty much ended rice farming forever for many planters. At the time, weather warnings were still limited, and there was virtually no evacuation, so residents and late-summer tourists alike suffered through the fearful storm.

**ERNESTO:** The first hurricane of the 2006 season, this storm dumped heavy rains across the Lowcountry, eventually making landfall on the North Carolina coast.

## EXTREME HURRICANE OF 1813:

In the centuries when there was no way to predict a hurricane, no watches or warnings and no mandatory evacuations, there was also no real way to calculate the "category" of a storm. However, the 1813 storm that hit the Lowcountry from north Florida to the North Carolina border was eventually deemed an "extreme hurricane" by a U.S. Weather Bureau chief meteorologist and director of the National Hurricane Center. Likewise, it was difficult to ascertain the financial damage, although in Charleston alone, it was estimated to be at least $22 million. Even the number of deaths was unknown for this hurricane, but was considered substantial and heartbreaking. Not all were as lucky as Major General John Floyd, an Indian fighter and commander of the Georgia militia during the War of 1812, who did not hear until weeks later that his wife and 12 children had indeed survived the "extreme hurricane."

**FABIAN:** September 2, 2003, this hurricane caused one drowning in rip currents near Cape Hatteras, North Carolina.

**FLORENCE:** In September 2000, this storm created rip currents that drowned three people in North Carolina.

**FLOYD:** Beginning as a tropical wave off Africa, this storm soon blossomed into a 400-mile-wide Category Four storm with 155 mile-per-hour winds. The hurricane first struck Abaco and surrounding islands, then headed to the southeastern U.S. coast. More than one million people evacuated inland from Miami to Jacksonville, Florida. By September 15, 1999, *Floyd* was aimed at the Lowcountry. Recalling the horrors of *Hugo*, there was no reluctance by Georgia and South Carolina coastal residents to evacuate. The storm sat about 100 miles off the shoreline. Except for bands of rain and gusty winds, the greatest drama from *Floyd* was the aggravation of the bumper-to-bumper evacuation. Luckily, a cold front pushed the storm offshore. Nonetheless, the hurricane did finally make landfall at Cape Fear, North Carolina, then sped on up into New England. At least 57 people died, most from sudden flooding, in this "mild" hurricane.

**FLYING FISH, 1792:** This schooner couldn't catch a break. A hurricane caught up with it off the Florida coast. In spite of close-reefing the sails, the ship was shoved up the coast of Georgia into even more severe weather, so suddenly that the seven of the seventeen crew and passengers could not even get out of the cabin and drowned. Survivors clung to the upturned hull of the schooner. Brave souls swam beneath the ship to cut away the masts and rigging to right the boat. Even then, the *Flying Fish* had taken on so much water that she barely floated. Spars lashed across the forecastle were used to steer the ship. Over the course of a fearful and miserable week, one passenger died aboard. A heavy sea shoved three others overboard. After another fateful week adrift, the ship was spotted by the passing *Derdaurhafft*, and the remaining six drenched and exhausted sailors were saved. The storm, still not done with its devastation, roared ashore in South Carolina.

**FORT GREENE:** The whopper hurricane of 1804 proved a real doozie up and down the entire Lowcountry coast. Even a fort was not sufficient for safety against the galloping water and cascading rain. Stranded in Savannah, Lieutenant Piatt and five other soldiers believed they could hold forth on Cockspur Island. However, by morning, high water slammed the two-story tabby and wood fortification known as Fort Greene. At high tide, those seeking shelter in the wind- and water-blown structure were terrified. Soldiers, wives, children, and washerwomen—21 in total—moved to the second floor as the water entered the blockhouse. Water chased them as they then ascended to the roof. The surge was so powerful that it moved a 4,800-pound cannon more than 30 feet. At 1 p.m., the structure collapsed. Clinging to the roof, the petrified passengers of this floating makeshift raft (including an infant) struggled to survive. Alas, the roof blew to shreds. About half of its passengers were swept to sea; the rest grabbed onto what splinters of wood they could reach. A few managed to hold on until they washed ashore. One was swept into a treetop and survived. Indeed, the entire island was awash. You may know the rebuilt fort today as Fort Pulaski!

*Tree damage can shut roads for days, even weeks, and allow water into structures; it all may look sort of innocent, but water, wind and duking it out with insurance companies is part of a painful aftermath of a storm.*

**FORTUNES LOST:** The enormous 1830 hurricane offers examples of the financial destruction wrought by such storms. In addition to the inevitable ruination of the land and loss of life, the destruction of crops and cargo and more produced an ill-fated future for those who had invested so much time, labor and money into planning and planting, securing, as best possible, ships and stores, and otherwise preparing for the hurricane season, which often struck just when crops were at their peak and about to be harvested. This particularly horrendous storm ruined endless cargo holds of sugar, rum, coffee, lumber, rice, cotton and more. On land, the sea island cotton crop was considered "a hopeless prospect." One planter described the St. Helena Island cotton as "…ruined by the gale. Scarce a green leaf is left, and what remains, bears the appearance of a field, that after caterpillars, or a heavy frost, had passed over it." "The corn is prostate and the potatoes much blighted," was the word from the sea islands of Hilton Head, Parris, Lemon, Daw's (Dataw) and Lady's. A planter on Crow Island at the North Santee River noted his entire rice crop was ruined, with the fields "red from the effects of salt water and wind." Twenty rice plantations on Winyah Bay and along the North and South Santee, Waccamaw, Black, Pee Dee and Sampit rivers were lost. Often, the destruction of goods and crops was so widespread and enormous that no financial total of the loss could be calculated, nor the cost to recover and start again.

**FRAN:** This September 6, 1996 hurricane was a Category Three. I know, since its 120 mile-per-hour winds spiraled over my oceanfront home in Emerald Isle, North Carolina, between Camp Lejeune and Morehead City. It was our second hurricane in 45 days, following the same path as *Bertha*. After *Bertha*, prisoners from Raleigh, the state capital, were sent down to walk the beach shoulder-to-shoulder to pick up debris. Our pool was filled with six feet of sand. The mean high tide water line was drastically changed, leaving some people without enough land to rebuild after their homes were destroyed. After *Fran*, no one came to help. The loose sand from the prior hurricane was picked up by the claw of this storm and slammed so deeply into oceanfront homes that we washed sand out of our shingles for the next two years. However, on the day we returned, the sun shone brightly, and it appeared that everyone lived in fairytale-like crystal castles. We sold our place and moved to…Colorado!

**FRANCES:** This 2004 hurricane crossed western North Carolina, dropping almost 24 inches of rain on Mount Mitchell. The resulting flooding of creeks and rivers damaged hundreds of homes and businesses.

**GASTON:** Just two weeks after hurricane *Charley*, *Gaston* came ashore in the Lowcountry on August 29, 2004. The slow-moving storm created many power outages, with 70 mile-per-hour winds pulling down lines and uprooting trees. Fishermen at Georgetown, South Carolina, kept their boat motors in gear to stop the surging tide from crashing their vessels on the wharf.

**GENERAL NICHOLS, 1797:** Hurricane season was always a period of great concern to sea captains and slave traders. On September 8, 1797, after a summer parade of tropical storms, a heavy gale began to pester the New Providence ship, the *General Nichols*. Headed for Savannah, the ship held a cargo of 150 slaves. After the hurricane caught Captain Michael Morrison unawares, the ship foundered. The crew launched a long boat and yawl, and was saved. However, 122 men, women and children—chained together below decks—went down with the ship. Those in the long boat survived for 24 hours until picked up by the schooner *Exuma*. The yawl and its occupants were never seen again.

**GEORGETOWN, 1834:** Yet another hurricane struck this vulnerable part of the Lowcountry, just north of Charleston. Just four years earlier, virtually all the crops here had been destroyed, and now, just as recovery was being made, this storm tore through, pushing saltwater inland as far as "the eye could reach." It was said,"...the fields were covered, and...we could not have known that valuable plantations lay under the overwhelming waters."

**GEORGIA BIGHT:** From the "Graveyard of the Atlantic" off North Carolina's Outer Banks to Florida's Cape Canaveral, this recess in the coastline has been believed to protect the Lowcountry from hurricanes. History has proven this is not true. The low-lying wetlands and the natural corridor that sucks hurricanes up the coast actually increases the destructibility factor of tropical storms and hurricanes, even those that do not actually make landfall.

**GORDON:** Extra tropical remnants of this storm tracked through North Carolina with light to moderate rainfall in September 2000.

**GRACIE:** It was 1959, September 29 to be exact. It had been five years since a hurricane had come ashore in the Lowcountry. Fickle *Gracie* pulled a fast one. First, it wandered about the Florida coast for days. Next, it was downgraded to a tropical storm. Just when everyone breathed a sigh of relief that the storm seemed headed to sea and oblivion, *Gracie* played a trick. She suddenly gained intensity, made a turn, and headed toward Charleston, South Carolina. By this time in hurricane history, events looked a lot more familiar: the mad race to the grocery store, storm shelters opening, the boarding up of homes and businesses, the closing of schools.

Aircraft and ships were moved upriver, to safer moorings or out to sea. Low-lying areas were evacuated. With maximum winds at 125 miles per hour, *Gracie* plunged ashore just north of Beaufort, South Carolina. At least 90 percent of telephone poles were blown down, many live oaks were uprooted like weeds, and homes and businesses damaged or destroyed. The mayor noted, "We won't be the same in 100 years." At Edisto Island, three-fourths of the pier washed away. The 200 people who chose to "ride out the storm" at Folly Beach found themselves cut off from the mainland. Charleston County suffered through the hurricane. Relentless *Gracie* then charged inland all the way to Columbia, the state capital.

**GREAT COASTAL HURRICANE OF 1806:** A mere two years after the devastating hurricane of 1804, this whopper struck the Lowcountry. The sailing ship *Rose-in-Bloom* was its worst victim. [See that entry on page 133.] However, the powerful storm also wrecked vessels all along the coast from St. Marys and Jekyll Island, Georgia, to Charleston and Georgetown, South

Carolina. Even the lighthouse at the entrance to Winyah Bay was blown down. Worse, this was just the beginning of yet another cycle of devastating Lowcountry hurricanes.

**"GREAT DROUGTH" HURRICANE OF 1752:** For 20 days the temperatures had hovered between 90 and 101 degrees in Charles Town. By early September, a hurricane was off St. Augustine, Florida, and growing in strength with every breath. Cumberland, Georgia's southernmost and largest barrier island, was the first to be hit. Fort William was demolished. Skies were called "cloudy and boisterous." The storm soon came ashore between Savannah and Charles Town as a major hurricane. Coming in on a lunar high tide, the wind and rains were referred to as "violent." The storm surge was 17 feet high. At least 40 large ships were ruined. Cannons and gun carriages were ripped off brick walls. As the sea poured into homes, the only way residents saved themselves was to swim to safety. One family escaped by hopping aboard an unmoored boat. Some families, along with servants and slaves, drowned. A ship filled with German immigrants was pummeled into the marsh so violently that 20 passengers died of severely broken limbs and other injuries. On Sullivan's Island, many people took refuge in the quarantine station, which the storm surge soon collapsed. By the end of the storm, more than 500 homes had been destroyed, along with so many pine trees that the tar export market went into great decline.

**GREAT HURRICANE OF 1713:** The storm was said to have come upon Charles Towne suddenly. The town was especially filled with residents and visitors who had fled there for protection with the outbreak of the Yemasee Indian War. A cresting tide was swept into the town by high winds and many lives were lost. The storm surge washed away many homes filled with settlers. New city walls, fortifications and an 80-foot lookout tower on Sullivan's Island were blown down. Following the storm, pirates, revolution and disease plagued the wounded town.

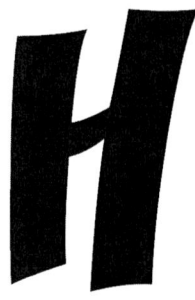

**HALLOWEEN HURRICANE, 1792:** As always, once the traditional period of hurricane activity begins to pass, we let down our guard a bit—always a big mistake. Surely the season was past, Lowcountry folk believed; surely enough was enough for one season. But on October 30, 1792, the winds and rain began; by Halloween, a full-blown hurricane was a'brew offshore. A "severe gale" morphed into "great violence." There was great fear of inundation, but the storm hit at low tide. Although it caused extensive damage, as is almost always noted, "It could have been worse!"

**HANNAH:** September 5, 2008…this hurricane moved ashore near the South Carolina/North Carolina border. While it packed strong winds and torrential rains, damage was minor.

**HAZEL:** Nicknamed "The Lady," *Hazel* 1954 was no lady! The storm first struck Haiti with winds over 100 miles-per-hour, where it killed hundreds. Because it then headed northward on an erratic coast, it was difficult to predict landfall, and thus, no evacuations were ordered. The sneaky storm suddenly showed its hand and blasted ashore at Ocean Drive near Myrtle Beach, South Carolina. The town siren blared and hurricane flags were belatedly hoisted. At least there was radio, and the U.S. Coast Guard was active in warnings. It was dire: a full moon, high tide, night coming on, raging winds, little advance warning, no evacuations to speak of, and *Hazel*, as it would turn out, was a "big one." Catastrophic in force, the storm straddled the North and South Carolina border. Forty-foot sand dunes were reduced to sea level; a new inlet was cut right through the end of Pawley's Island. With 200 homes gone and the rest damaged, all was described as "a debris of destruction." Waves of 40-50 feet high overwhelmed Ocean Drive Beach. The future "Grand Strand" was anything but after the storm sped through, pretty much gouging, shoving, clawing or drowning most everything it encountered—$184 million (in today's dollars) worth of damage. So powerful was the storm, some folks found their refrigerators (and lots of other stuff) as far as three miles inland. Surprisingly, there was only a single death in South Carolina. North Carolina had 150 mile-per-hour winds, 19 storm-related fatalities, and damage worth almost $1 billion in today's dollars—*Hazel* is still the most powerful hurricane to hit the state, to date. The vicious storm pressed on into Virginia and the northeastern U.S., not satisfied until it had done all the damage possible. More than 100 died. This catastrophic storm was truly one of historic proportions, and not surprisingly, is still talked about as a momentous Lowcountry event.

**HILTON HEAD ISLAND:** Shaped like a shoe, with its long sole facing the sea, this island has often been stomped by hurricanes. In 2016, *Matthew* clobbered the island badly, wreaking havoc on Harbor Town, as well as many of the plantations. Thousands of trees were toppled, and the resulting destruction to property was in the millions of dollars. Residents were not allowed back on the island for days, and this area was among the last in the county to have power restored.

**HMMM...:** While early reports of the New World touted a place of great beauty and resources, brave settlers, who came with some fear and trepidation to the Lowcountry, soon became "terrified and fearful" of the heat that led to severe storms in late summer and early autumn. From rich planters to ordinary citizens to lowly slaves and servants, all felt dread at an impending hurricane. That there was no real warning and no insight as to possible landfall place or time, added to the foreboding. Summer, indeed, was a regular period of heat, disease and slam-dunk storms. That homes were insubstantial did not help matters; most of the time, even brick fortifications did not survive. Storm surge was more experienced than understood. Few preparations, if any, or precautions were taken prior to storms. Ships often lay at sea or simply anchored at harbor. It gave pause to those often eager to migrate to this area, and further consternation if they chose to do so. Many would-be immigrants avoided the area altogether. A word to the wise who had survived an actual hurricane was sufficient to give pause…hmmm, this does not seem so true today?

**HOME:** In the still gnarly seas following the twin hurricanes of 1837, a great tragedy occurred that affected many Lowcountry residents and led to a new, crucial law in shipping. The steamship *Home* left New York City for Charleston. Aboard were 90 passengers and around 40 officers and crew. The families had gone north to escape the summer heat and were now returning, confident that the serious storms of the season had passed. However, the *Home* found itself on a collision course with a slow-moving hurricane. Off the North Carolina coast, the ship began to leak, water ankle deep in the hold and rising. By morning "the sea raged frightfully," one passenger noted. As the hurricane held the vessel tight, its paddle wheel caught more air than water and the *Home* pitched and rolled. When the pumps failed to hold, the entire crew, as well as all able passengers, were set to bailing. The monstrous seas sent water into the boilers. When that water extinguished the fire, the captain's plan to beach the ship was thwarted. Just off Cape Hatteras—in the fearsome Graveyard of the Atlantic—the *Home* struck a sandbar. It was just 100 yards from shore, but it might as well have been miles. Waves crashed onto the deck of the ship, now level with the water, and washed many passengers into the sea to their deaths. One mother jumped into the ocean to save the child that had just been swept from her arms; both drowned. A lifeboat was set adrift with some passengers aboard, but it capsized and all died. Clinging desperately to what remained of the ship, more terrified women, children and men were flung into the roiling water. The captain, who had been at the helm for hours, was drenched with seawater, yet continued to try to save his ship and passengers. While he eventually reached the shore, most were not so fortunate. One woman had been tied to a sturdy piece of wood and was washed ashore. Another woman had been strapped to a sofa and finally surfed up onto the sand with the help of others. Only 20 of 90 passengers survived; about half the crew made it to safety. A year after this major maritime Lowcountry disaster, the U.S. Congress passed a law requiring commercial vessels to carry a life preserver for each passenger.

**HUGO-I:** This hurricane, of course, is in a class of its own. Assumed to be the most destructive and costly storm in the history of the Lowcountry, *Hugo* began in thunderstorms off the Senegal coast in West Africa in September 1989. By September 11, it had been upgraded to a tropical cyclone and given a name that would become memorable in South Carolina hurricane history. As a Category Four, the storm gained winds of 130-155 miles per hour and soon scoured the Caribbean, leaving 44 dead and massive destruction in its wake. Now deemed a "killer storm," *Hugo* made its move toward the southeastern coast of the U.S. On September 20 and 21, the storm tracked toward Savannah, Georgia. The National Hurricane Center in Coral Gables, Florida, announced there was a 21 percent chance that the storm would make landfall at Savannah or Charleston. Georgians fled inland, but the storm skidded past with little damage and fairly low winds. But soon, *Hugo* was off the coast of Charleston, a Category Four, and spiraling winds of 135 miles-per-hour. The storm was the size of the entire state of South Carolina, mostly still hanging off the coast, out to sea. The governor ordered a mandatory evacuation of all coastal areas. Emergency shelters were opened. Throughout the day, fairly moderate winds brushed Hilton Head, Beaufort and St. Helena Island. Then, around 9:00 p.m., the dangerous right front quadrant of the storm began to strike.

**HUGO-II:** Folly Beach, Charleston, Mount Pleasant, Sullivan's Island, Isle of Palms, Awendaw, McClellanville—all were in danger. The first winds broke gas lines and caused electrical transformers to burst into flames. By 10:30 p.m. the winds reached 90 miles per hour with gusts up to 130. Hard, horizontal rain began to yank off pieces of slate, tin, and copper from the roofs of buildings. They soon became projectiles that burst into automobile windshields and plate glass windows of storefronts, shops, and public buildings. Even the roofs of emergency shelters were swept away, forcing evacuations to other shelters. City Hall was in darkness, where the mayor and other town officials tried to manage the crisis while also saving valuable historical paintings from water damage. It was a fearful evening as people hunkered down, listening to the sound of huge oaks crashing and utility poles snapping. Bursts of fire raged from natural gas leaks. Radio and television stations went off the air. Then around midnight, a 20-foot storm surge rolled over historic Fort Sumter in Charleston Harbor, and all hell broke loose.

**HUGO-III:** Boats and ships of all sizes were dismasted, smashed into docks, or blown into the marsh into one nautical mess. About 80 percent of homes at Folly Beach, inundated by the storm surge, were destroyed or suffered great damage. Damage was equally as severe at Mount Pleasant, Sullivan's Island and the Isle of Palms. You might think that everyone this close to the coast would have evacuated, but one man who had erected elaborate sand and fence defenses discovered them immediately washed away, his home and its contents spilled from the split house and littered the beach. Others, enjoying a "hurricane party," fled when their home began to break apart. Every fishing pier for more than 100 miles was washed away. When the eye of the hurricane passed overhead around 1:00 a.m., you could zip outdoors and perhaps see concrete and steel bridges damaged so much that access was cut off from one Charleston community to another. After a quick glimpse, you'd best scurry back inside before the next onslaught of wind and rain. Again, you'd think most folks would have evacuated, but way too many found themselves trapped in condos or apartment buildings. One woman stood on her kitchen counter as she watched her refrigerator begin to float, while yet others quickly fashioned makeshift life jackets for themselves and their pets as they watched the water rise. Some unwisely tried to move their boats to safety, or use them as shelter, and drowned. Swank historic homes on the Battery got as wet as shanty homes on the riverbanks. Heroes emerged even in the midst of the storm: two men tied ropes around their waists and waded into deep water to man a pump and keep power coming to a hospital's emergency room. Non-heroic looters clambered into shops where wind or water had bashed in windows, leaving goods easy pickings. Many people clung to anything they could to keep their heads above the rising waters; some climbed onto the tallest furnishings on the second floors of their homes, while others hung from rafters until the waters receded.

**HUGO-IV:** The tiny fishing village of McClellanville endured a singular story that fearsome night. With 400 residents, the people who lived on the edge of the Cape Romaine seashore near Bull's Bay were more than knowledgeable about storms. They just didn't know that they would get the right front quadrant of the storm around their necks once the eye passed, 140 mile-per-hour winds, and a storm surge from hell. Villagers said later that the hurricane sounded like a freight train. If *Hugo* was powerful enough to toss 70-foot trawlers about, what hope was there for men, women and children? Homes filled with water, washed off their foundations, or out to sea. People blew away. Toilets backed up with seawater. A mile away, across Highway 17, a woman opened her door to see ocean waves headed her way. In the shelter at Lincoln High School, people panicked when water poured in and forced them onto tables, then onto the stage, and some onto the roof. A new 100-foot-wide channel was cut right through Pawley's Island. More than 50,000 truckloads of sand washed right off Myrtle Beach—their just-completed beach renourishment project reduced to a slick tabletop. More than 100 public access walkways made of thick concrete slabs were destroyed. Indeed, statistics that showed the fury of *Hugo* were rampant: 60% of the endangered red-cockaded woodpecker population died; 70% of trees in some places—even inland—split, toppled, and fell; and it was estimated that one million board feet of timber was lost. *Hugo* was over, but the primary statistic left was that this was the worse storm to hit the Lowcountry and the state of South Carolina. Damages easily totaled more than $1 billion.

**HUMAN TRAGEDY:** The 1835 September hurricane in the Lowcountry took one of those surprise spirals across Florida into the Gulf of Mexico, then back across Florida to Georgia and South Carolina. It was said that limbs were ripped from the trees. Like so many of the 1800 storms, this hurricane wreaked havoc of all the usual sorts, but what often is not recorded among the statistics of ship and crop loss or the numbers of structures destroyed or even lives lost, are the sad details. In this storm, for example, at the Port Royal Ferry, near Beaufort, the mail boy and his horse, sticking to their duties, drowned when the wind blew them into the sea.

**HUMBERTO:** In 2007, the remnants of this North Carolina hurricane dropped rainfall all the way into the Appalachian Mountains.

**HURRICANE:** From the native Caribbean word *hurracan*, or evil spirit. A hurricane is basically a huge storm. One can span 600 miles across and have winds that spiral inward and upward at speeds of 75-200 miles per hour, and pour down literally more than 2.4 trillion gallons of rain. Hurricanes usually last for more than a week and move 10-20 miles per hour over the open ocean. They gather heat and energy through contact with warm seawater. Hurricanes generally lose strength once they move over land. However, they can regain strength if they track back over open water.

**HUTCHINSON ISLAND, GEORGIA:** Today, most of us know Hutchinson Island, across the Savannah River from River Street, as the home of the Westin Hotel and the lovely Savannah Harbor Golf Club. However, in the 1804 hurricane, it was the site of many drownings. In the 1824 equally horrendous hurricane, everyone was evacuated, often at great risk and peril. The night of September 14, the Back and Savannah Rivers joined forces to overwash the island. Plantation houses and rice crops were devastated by the high wind and water. The Union Ferry Wharf washed away, and ships collided and sunk. Across the river in Savannah, scores of the beautiful live oaks that adorned the squares crashed to the earth. Several houses at Yamacraw Bluff were blown down. The jail, stores, historic homes and warehouses were damaged. It was always common in a strong hurricane that chimneys crashed into homes and slate shingles sling-shotted in the air like missiles. Elba Island, today the site of the gas tanks, in the middle of the Savannah River, was home to the Shad family. Their plantation, outbuildings and crops were all washed away. Their slaves only survived by climbing into the rafters of the overseer's house. The storm was so powerful that it roared all the way up to Augusta, leaving much damage in its wake. More than 1,600 wagonloads of demolished Pride of India trees were hauled off after the storm. Across the river in South Carolina, Beaufort was badly battered. The May River flooded to ruin unpicked crops. Every bridge between the Combahee River and Purysburg was destroyed, as were bridges at Tulifinny and Pocataligo. At Edisto, it was said that stalks of cotton were stripped bare. The hateful hurricane persistently made its way on up into Charleston, and after scouring that town, hit Georgetown. No Lowcountry lowland, delta, town or rural burg was left unscathed. Twelve hurricanes had hit the Lowcountry between 1800 and 1824, and residents were weary, often financially ruined, suffered other losses, and quite generally demoralized. Some, fed up, broke, and sick of the incessant onslaught, moved away.

# I

**IDA:** It may have been just the remnants of a hurricane, but it still did a lot of damage in the Lowcountry and along the rest of the U.S. East Coast.

**IGOR:** A surfer died in strong waves at Surf City, North Carolina, in this September 2011 hurricane.

**IRENE:** This hurricane made landfall at Cape Lookout, North Carolina, as a strong Category One storm, killing seven and doing severe wind and flood damage on August 27, 2011.

**ISABEL:** On September 18, 2003, *Isabel* made landfall at Drum Inlet, North Carolina, with winds of 105 miles per hour. Three deaths occurred. Of the $450 million in damage, most was in Dare County, where many homes washed away. The storm surge created a 2,000-foot-wide inlet on Hatteras Island, which isolated Hatteras by road for two months.

**ISADORE:** In September 2002, the large wind field of what was once this hurricane downed trees and power lines in western North Carolina.

*Hurricane Hugo dismantles Ben Sawyer Bridge to Sullivan's Island.*

**ISLE OF PALMS, SOUTH CAROLINA:** Following the devastating hurricane of 1911, one of the fatalities was South Carolina's lucrative rice cultivation. Long an economic mainstay of the Lowcountry, many planters sold off their rice plantations, croplands and threshing mills. The ripple effect of losing this historic commodity was seen in many ways, ranging from reduced shipping to loss of jobs. "Carolina Gold" was now more like coastal sand, blown to sea, never to return.

**ITALIAN VESSEL NOE:** Off Tybee Island, Georgia, during the 1898 hurricane, sat the 512-ton Italian bark *Noe*. That is until the forceful winds blew the ship around where it began to be smashed to smithereens by the powerhouse waves. The sailors climbed into the rigging, so fearful were they of being swept overboard. Indeed, one sailor grabbed a life vest and jumped overboard, then immediately drowned. After witnessing the disaster, the local U.S. Corps of Engineers ventured out with a small sailboat and five men to try to save the Italian sailors. The lieutenant thrust his West Point ring and wallet to a bystander, saying, "Keep these for me, one can't tell what may happen." The rescue boat soon encountered serious breakers along the sandbar between it and the *Noe*. Instead of heading out of harm's way, the crew pressed on. Suddenly, a giant wave hit the sailboat and capsized it. Now on the sandbar, the men held on to the boat, yet yanked off most of their clothes to avoid being weighed down in the high surf. All but the lieutenant, that is; and so, when the next large wave broke on the bar, it sucked him into the sea. Another rescuer soon drowned. The remaining three held to the small craft as they were pushed and shoved by the sea for five long hours toward Daufuskie Island. The men were saved when they finally washed ashore. The sailors on the *Noe* were eventually rescued. Their ship finally came aground at Daufuskie as well; both craft were a total loss. The two drowned men were apparently never seen again.

**IVAN:** In 2004, this hurricane tracked along the border of North Carolina and Tennessee, dropping more than 17 inches of rain and spawning 4 tornadoes. Eight people were killed. Many bridges were washed away and hundreds of homes and stores damaged.

**JEANNE:** A man was thrown overboard from his boat and drowned in this 2004 hurricane. Three days later, the remnants of the storm caused the third hurricane-related flooding in western North Carolina in a month.

**JEKYLL ISLAND, GA:** An 1804 hurricane made landfall virtually simultaneously at this barrier island, as well as at Cumberland and St. Simons Islands. Most of Jekyll was inundated, decimating the lucrative sea island cotton crop.

**JOAQUIN:** This unique hurricane, occurring in October 2015, created a 1,000-year flood in and around the inland state capital of Columbia, South Carolina. Heavy flooding also hit Charleston all the way up to rural Williamsburg County in Virginia. More than two feet of rain fell on Columbia the weekend of October 3. More than 16 inches fell in one 24-hour period. Nine people drowned in Columbia. The storm caused over $2 billion in damage to homes, businesses, dams, and other structures. This area is still recovering.

*This is why you don't seek shelter in a boat during a hurricane.*

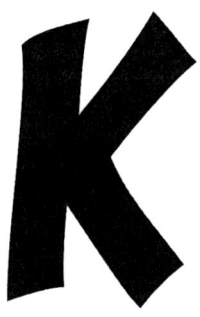

**KATRINA:** In August 2005, this excruciatingly powerful Category Five storm that destroyed so much of New Orleans and killed so many, dumped rains in the Lowcountry. Many refugees from the Louisiana disaster flooded into Georgia, the Carolinas and beyond. The parade of utility trucks and other helpers filled the interstate highways as they headed to provide disaster aid and relief. The best book to read about this national disaster is *The Great Deluge* by Douglas Brinkley, historian and New Orleans resident.

**KIAWAH ISLAND, SOUTH CAROLINA:** In the Great Hurricane of 1752, almost 50 people on this island barely survived a massive storm surge by rushing into an old corn house on pilings, which swayed mightily until the waters receded.

**KLAUS:** This 1990 minor hurricane eventually reached the coast of South Carolina. However, the damage that it did (primarily in the Caribbean) along its path to oblivion, caused its name to be retired from the national hurricane list. This storm did delay the launch of a space shuttle. There had also been a hurricane *Klaus* in 1984.

**KNOCK-A-BOUT HURRICANE OF 1894:** This hurricane caught weather bureaus off guard, so there was little warning of this storm that seemed to just want to knock everyone and everything off their feet. It first came ashore on Florida's Gulf Coast, then took what we now know as that overland express right to the Lowcountry, sort of in our back door. St. Marys, Folkston, Waycross and Woodbine, Georgia, had stores, hotels and homes blown all about, killing a black barber. The elementary school was considered the strongest building in town, but it collapsed with 38 children and a teacher inside; fortunately none were injured. In this big timber area, the flying trees proved to be horrid projectiles, actually piercing homes.

One person described the former forests as a "prairie" after the storm. The turpentine industry suffered a loss equal to $10 million dollars today. At the port of Brunswick, many people were hurt, and the church, school, grain silos, opera house, and more were destroyed. The pier, cottages, hotel and churches were severely damaged or destroyed at St. Simon's. It was said no building escaped damage at Darien. On up the coast, Tybee Island was knocked about by the hurricane. Savannah's port had ships large and small shoved ashore and a number of deaths. Half the trees in lovely Forsyth Park were blown down. The storm then roared up the entire South Carolina coast doing similar damage. After the storm finally passed, many complained about the lack of warning. Although deemed a very severe hurricane, the winds were not particularly high (meaning some were a mere 60 miles per hour), and it struck at low tide. But the evidence seems clear that warnings and evacuation are important since you truly cannot know what a hurricane might do—each seems to have a mind of its own.

**KYLE:** This 2002 hurricane was the fifth-longest-lived Atlantic hurricane, initiating on September 20, looping, wandering, and otherwise oscillating for another 22 days until it made landfalls near Charleston, South Carolina, and Long Beach, North Carolina. Its worst damage in the Lowcountry was at Georgetown, South Carolina, where 106 buildings were damaged, 7 destroyed, and 8 people injured. *Kyle* was also the source of four tornadoes.

**LADY'S ISLAND, SC:** An 1827 hurricane laid low the sea islands here. A few quotes say it all: The storm "prostrated the hopes of the planter." "Cotton is ruined… Scarce a green leaf is left, and what remains, bears the appearance of a field, that after caterpillars, or a heavy frost, had passed over it." "…cotton is battered and bruised…" "The corn is all prostrate and the potatoes much blighted."

**"LASHED TO THE AFTER-HOUSE":** What could be more fearsome than to be lashed to a ship to avoid being lost at sea? That's what happened when the powerful 1873 hurricane knocked over the schooner *Sylvan*. The captain ordered the five crewmen to lash themselves to the after-house, which they did. An enormous wave then tore off the after-house and the attached crew. For three days they drifted without food or water, nearly naked, exhausted, and losing hope, but were rescued by a passing schooner.

## LAST STORM OF THE CENTURY—

**I:** A major hurricane struck the Lowcountry on October 2, 1898. The first damage was offshore on the high seas. A brig out of Brunswick, Georgia, had its steward washed overboard and the remaining crew not rescued for three long days. Off Charleston, an 880-ton Norwegian bark was capsized, tossing all the crew overboard. The captain tied his legs to a floating piece of the ship and held on for a three-day rollercoaster ride from hell aboard his makeshift raft. Although he was drifting alone in open sea, he was headed toward the coast. At last, a fishing smack rescued him, the lone survivor of the *Safir*. Two sailors washed ashore at Edisto Island, South Carolina, after their schooner, filled with 1,800 tons of phosphate rock, sunk. They were the only survivors of the *Sarah E. Palmer*. *The Wandering Jew*, stuffed with 1,000 tons of coal, foundered off the Isle of Palms. As the ship tore apart, the sailors took refuge in the rigging and were later rescued "just in the nick of time."

**LAST STORM OF THE CENTURY-II:** This powerful 1898 hurricane of super high winds and towering waves scoured Fernandina Beach, Florida; then headed up to St. Marys, Georgia, where it dumped "the greatest tidal wave in the history of the town." Next, the storm made landfall at Cumberland Island as a Category 4 hurricane. The storm surge flooded the great Carnegie mansion there, as well as a fine yacht. Waves drove sailing ships into a sandbar, where eight sailors drowned. The 20-foot storm surge plowed into other sea islands, washing away the fort at Jekyll Island and even dismounting heavy cannon. Many of the "millionaires' cottages" suffered a wash-through of water, with the dock of the Jekyll Island Club coming to rest on the cottage of Joseph Pulitzer. The town of Brunswick suffered 18 straight hours of hard rain and wind. That Thomas Spaulding complained, "The hurricane was so sudden. It came up and you didn't know what hit you," was proof that warnings were still sparse.

**LAST STORM OF THE CENTURY-III:** As a Category 4 storm, the 1898 hurricane swept water out of the bay, river and creeks. Brunswick was inundated. Hundreds of thousands of feet of lumber, hundreds of railroad cross-ties, and many barrels of naval stores were washed off the docks. The wind was so fierce that some residents found themselves pinned to walls when they tried to escape homes or shops and make a run for it. Others escaped in small boats on the rivers of water rushing down all the streets of the town. Some men swam—knives in their mouths—to the town stables to free the horses tethered there. Twenty were rescued and given shelter in the Baptist church. The mean shanties of the African Americans were especially hard hit and numerous people drowned, including children. After a mini-riot of unruly and desperate residents, ending with a shooting and a knifing, there was nothing to do—the jail was filled with four feet of water. The sea covered almost all of St. Simons. Endless old oaks fell, "their limbs crossed and recrossed." "Dead animals lie plentifully around." And "all the pretty cottages" were "piled in one inextricable mass..." On Egg Island and in the rice field areas, the death toll was extensive, all African American.

**LAST STORM OF THE CENTURY-IV:** Coming in on a high tide and a full moon, this hurricane was a tragic disaster for so many in 1898. The tidal surge at Butler's Island drowned 80 black men, women and children. The lighthouse keeper on Sapelo Island swore a 33-foot wave hit the lighthouse. As waves beat his house to pieces, the man swam with one child after the other to safety in the lighthouse. On Doboy Island, one family survived by opening their front and back doors to let the storm surge rush through. As the storm rushed on up the coast, the winds began to subside somewhat until the last hurricane in this century fizzled out, much to the relief of exhausted and frustrated Lowcountrians, their lives and the economy left in weary tatters.

**"LONGEST CONTINUOUS BLOW":** That's what many Charleston area residents said of the major 1854 hurricane. More than

$6 million in wharves were destroyed along Bay Street alone. Numerous ships blew into one another or ashore, many so far inland as to be quite difficult to retrieve. Causeways and bridges were washed out. The elegant Charleston Hotel and many of the historic, swank homes lost roofs, exposing the luxurious interiors to wind and rain. Seawater covered Sullivan's Island. More than 1,000 islanders fled to Fort Moultrie to avoid being drowned. This humongous storm clawed its way up the Georgia Bight. It was remembered by local media as the "longest continuous blow in the memory of any inhabitant."

**LOOTING:** Vandalism, looting, plundering, stealing—all have been part of hurricanes as long as there has been anything left behind or unprotected. After the 1752 hurricane in Charles Town, South Carolina, the militia was called out to prevent looting, protect property, and arrest those who took advantage of the calamity. While it is tempting to stay during a hurricane to guard your property, don't.

**LOWCOUNTRY HURRICANES:** Like that famed "butterfly effect," storms that eventually pound the Lowcountry begin as a seed of wind, often as far away as Africa. The rise of massive amounts of water vapor forms ever-denser cumulus clouds. Rainstorms, thunder and lightning result. If the recipe is right—barometric pressure drops and the earth's rotation creates a counterclockwise movement—a tropical depression is born. Spiraling winds swirl around an area of low pressure and are shoved along by trade winds. Traveling over warm seawater, more moisture and heat fuel higher winds and precipitation. Clouds may climb to ten miles high. When wind speeds reach 39 miles per hour, the tropical depression becomes a tropical storm.

While we peck away at computers in Charleston, this tropical storm may intensify into an empty core belted by bands of rain. As we sleep late on a Saturday morning, the storm may speed up its rotation and the barometric pressure may continue to fall. At a wind speed of 74 miles per hour, the storm is deemed a hurricane.

We may spy the interruption of a weather crawl beneath the Clemson-South Carolina game before we become aware that a hurricane is on the move. We may be unconcerned. After all, hurricanes are unpredictable and often head in directions that mean no threat to us. But, as with the recent *Matthew*, once a hurricane sets its course and stays on it, the storm may bear down with vengeance in all manner of ways. Some remain offshore, spitting squalls our way; others make a beeline right to the most vulnerable part of our Lowcountry geography. Some play trickster and squirm around a bit, keeping us off guard. Fearsome at any time, hurricanes were especially horrific before accurate weather forecasts. Yet, even today, with 24/7 weather reports of great specificity, the Lowcountry— at or near sea level—remains one of the most vulnerable places a hurricane can hit.

**MATTHEW-I:** This, the 13th named storm, 5th hurricane, and 2nd major hurricane of the 2016 Atlantic season, was born from a tropical wave off the coast of Africa on September 22. It soon became a tropical storm, then quickly intensified to hurricane status, blossoming into a Category Five storm for a short while. By the time it hit Haiti on October 4, it was a Category Four hurricane of widespread destruction and death. After leaving Haiti, it simmered down to a Category Three, then revved back up to a Category Four. This was certainly a very powerful, deadly storm with a long life. And it was headed to the Lowcountry.

**MATTHEW-II:** Here in the Lowcountry, we were somewhat in denial. The "It can't happen here" mode let us go on about our business during some beautiful Indian summer weather. But when the storm moved 100 miles westward, everyone quickly began to take notice. Since it had been so long since a hurricane had made a direct hit along the South Carolina/Georgia border, many folks assumed that the storm would veer off, weaken, or perhaps just be an insignificant tropical storm similar to one that had balmily passed through just a few weeks earlier. Instead, *Matthew* kept coming. Everyone could argue how close it might come, whether it would be a One or a Two, and how convenient, even fun, it might be to stay and "ride it out." But in Georgia and South Carolina, mandatory evacuations were announced for coastal areas. I live in Beaufort County, South Carolina, which has no storm shelters—which just shows the vulnerability of our low part of the Lowcountry. Some people chose to stay. Some left early, in hopes of crossing the Talmadge Bridge over the Savannah River, and to go where they wanted, on the roads they preferred. Others waited and ended up not only in bumper-to-bumper traffic, but passing service stations with no gasoline, and scrambling to find motel or hotel rooms. Some people chose to "shelter in place," as we call the foolhardy decision to stay and try to protect homes and businesses. Whatever decision you made, it was a moot point, for the storm was now coming.

**MATTHEW-III:** Preparations were underway all up and down the coast. States of emergency were declared…select interstates went into reverse lane mode…Port Canaveral, Florida, was closed by the U.S. Coast Guard for the first time since 2004, turning back cruise ships and cargo ships. For only the fourth time in its 45-year history, Walt Disney World was closed. Football games were canceled and rescheduled. Homes were boarded up, large glass windows taped, and supplies secured via long lines at gas stations, grocery stores, and hardware stores. Newscasts were "all hurricane" all the time. As *Matthew* marauded Haiti, then marched over the Dominican Republic, Cuba and the Bahamas, the Lowcountry watched, waited, worried, and, if smart, evacuated.

**MATTHEW-IV:** Although *Matthew* only edged along the coast of Florida, it left more than one million people without power. Parts of Highway A1A were washed out. The state experienced 12 deaths and millions of dollars in damage to the Kennedy Space Center. Off Jacksonville, the storm reduced in intensity from a Category Four to a Category Two storm. In Georgia, all roads to St. Simons Island were impassable, and 250,000 Georgians had no power. The storm then skirted over Daufuskie Island, Bluffton, Hilton Head, Beaufort, and headed up to Charleston. News reports from Savannah and Charleston failed to take into account the massive destruction in the wedge of Lowcountry in between. Thousands of trees, including many large live oaks festooned with Spanish moss, were downed. Roads were impassible to those trying to return after the storm. Hilton Head took a real beating, especially Sea Pines and a number of the plantations. Interstate 95 was closed in many sections due to flooding. The Waccamaw and Little Pee Dee rivers, on up the coast, reached record crests. Lumberton, North Carolina, had serious flooding; it was an area that some South Carolinians had evacuated to. Storm surge destroyed or damaged boats and homes. Schools were closed for the remainder of the week. At least 600,000 customers did not have power for days, if not weeks. The death toll in Florida was 12, Georgia 3, North Carolina 28, South Carolina 4, and Virginia 2. Total damage was at least $7-8 billion, with a final reckoning still to be determined since it would be 2017 before much of the damage was cleaned up.

*Hurricane Matthew hovers in the Atlantic Ocean, preparing to make a beeline for the Lowcountry.*

**MAY RIVER:** Those of us who know and love the beautiful river known as the May…

may believe that it is serene and well-behaved enough to mind its manners and stay below the fortunate level of its bluffs. However, in the 1804 hurricane—one of the wildest and wooliest ever to approach these shores—the river overflowed, filling and ruining magnificent rice and cotton crops and storage facilities, plantations and slave cabins. Nearby islands, such as Daufuskie, were also overwashed and lives lost.

**MCCLELLANVILLE, SOUTH CAROLINA:** An extremely low-lying fishing village, just north of Charleston, took the brunt of storm surge from *Hugo*. Hearty souls who did not evacuate had a moment of panic as the water filled their bolt-hole community center and children and adults alike clung to rafters until the water subsided enough for them to drop down to picnic tables.

**MORRIS:** Hurricanes are fickle; they care not who is rich, who is poor, who may be cowardly, or who may be wise and brave, who acts fast, or who may hesitate. During the awful Lowcountry hurricane of 1804, a slave named Morris saved the day. He was the "headman" of a gang of around 100 slaves who worked the crops of a planter on Little St. Simons Island, Georgia. As such, he was responsible for the men. With the humongous storm bearing down on them, the natural instinct of the men was to hasten back across the water to home. As they turned to flee for their rickety craft, Morris literally cracked the whip, the bullwhip of his authority, and ordered the slaves to take refuge instead in a large log structure built for just this kind of situation. Instead of likely drowning, the men were saved. To emphasize the danger, consider a parallel story taking place at the same time just an island away. The overseer here failed to take timely measures to herd the workers into an equally sturdy rice barn. The storm surge breached the rice embankments. Men, women and children, unable to cross the rising water, were swept out to sea. Their 70 bodies were never recovered.

**MOSQUITO FLEET:** Famous in Charleston history, "the Mosquito Fleet" consisted of a group of African American fishermen who supplied the city with much of its seafood needs. Almost every morning, the fleet left the harbor in their smacks and sloops for their usual fishing ground 25 miles out in the Atlantic Ocean. They did so on the day of September 13, 1904. For unknown reasons, the U.S. Weather Bureau had sent no warnings of an approaching hurricane. By the time the fleet reached the blackfish banks, they were in trouble. The waves were running "mountain high." The *Pride*, a 27-foot boat, headed back to port, but soon capsized, tossing all crew into the sea. Only one person survived. Many of the boats—*Big Ella*, *Gray Eagle*, *Dora*, *Salem*—foundered in the high seas. Admirably, captains and crew from each boat tried to help the other. Some were successful; others not so. The crew on one boat refused to take refuge on a larger vessel, requesting just a towline. The boat sank and the crew fell into the sea. Of the five who drowned, two had been previously rescued from another boat.

**"MOST STORMY AND DESTRUCTIVE SEASON":** Eleven hurricanes were spawned in the West Indies in 1837. In early August, one advance on the Lowcountry. Almost immediately, a number of ships—the *Eliza and Emma, Providence, Anna and Minerva, Mills, Ann and Bolivar, Florida,* and more—were smashed, foundered, capsized or sunk at wharf or offshore. The *Mills* became one of the worst maritime disasters on the Georgia coast, with only a single survivor who washed ashore at Jekyll Island. St. Marys was "six feet under" in water, and many residents fled in boats just ahead of their homes that soon washed away. Trees were stripped of their limbs and uprooted. Cotton and rice fields were inundated and destroyed. Every town from Savannah to Charleston came under the onslaught of this particularly hateful hurricane. However, this storm was only the beginning. Followed close on its receding heels was another equally strong hurricane. It hit in mid-August with a fury of "tremendous seas." Once more, ships—*Lovely Keizia* and *Martha Pyatt*—for examples, encountered treacherous weather, with often, all hands lost at sea. Captain Brown of the *David B. Crane* had to fight off the storm and a mutiny at the same time! The hurricane moved up the Georgia Bight, ripping away beaches. There was horrendous damage to homes, livestock and crops, even with the eye still offshore. The Lowcountry, from stem to stern, was basically exhausted from the rather constant parade of hurricanes. Many old-timers said they had never seen such destruction.

**MUTUAL SAFETY:** There was nothing mutual and nothing safe about this steamer caught up in an 1846 hurricane off the South Carolina and Georgia coast. So fierce was the wind that the upper deck had to be cut off and discarded and tossed into the sea in an attempt to keep the boat upright. Soon the crew had to intentionally ground the ship in a heavy surf, launch the lifeboats and row the women passengers ashore. As soon as all the passengers and crew were safely on shore, the waves defeated the ship, which sank.

**MYTHS:** "We can't have a hurricane here." "A hurricane never strikes the same place twice." "Hurricanes don't come back to back."

**NATIONAL HURRICANE CENTER:** The NHC is part of the National Centers for Environmental Prediction (NCEP), located in Miami, Florida. The Hurricane Specialist Unit (HSU) maintains a continuous watch on tropical cyclones and other weather disturbances in the North Atlantic and eastern North Pacific basins. The HSU prepares and issues analyses and forecasts. Other divisions include a Tropical Analysis and Forecast Branch, a Technology and Science Branch, The Storm Surge Unit, The Chief Aerial Reconnaissance Coordination, All Hurricanes unit, and The Hurricane Liaison Team. With all these looking out for us, I still remember Bob Sheets, when he was head of the NHC, keeping us posted on national television, even as his own home blew away, during *Andrew*. These folks take hurricanes seriously.

## NEW CENTURY HURRICANE, 1804:

The new century came into the colonial Lowcountry with a bang, or, rather, a blow. The first hint of trouble was a "very severe squall" that struck the Gulf Stream off Savannah in late August. In spite of the captain's decision to "let fly tacks, sheets, and halyards," the packet *Alexander* capsized "in an instant." All souls were nearly lost after a week of great danger and deprivation; rescue in the nick of time (for most of the crew) came from the passing *Olive*. Fairly simultaneously, a "violent hurricane" was sweeping across Jamaica. This marked the beginning of one of the worst hurricane seasons the Lowcountry had ever experienced. Taking out ports and ships as it marched east and northward, the storm gathered strength and made a beeline for the Lowcountry. Lashing out at St. Augustine, leaving only ten ships afloat in the harbor, the hurricane soon overcame the entire Georgia and South Carolina coast. No point was left unscathed: St. Marys...Tybee Island...Savannah...Charleston...and all in between were caught up in the maelstrom, whether offshore, on the coast, or inland. Coming north to south, or south to north, ships found themselves in turmoil, foundered, and sunk. Cargo ranging from rum, soap, Negro cloth, and more, adorned the sea bed. While the names of many of the distressed vessels were recorded—*Betsy, Phoebe, Liberty, Experiment,* and others—the names and numbers of the dead are unknown.

**NIGHT STORM, 1770:** Those who have been through a hurricane know that one that strikes after dark is the most frightening. This hurricane bore down upon Savannah and the Carolinas as a "great storm at night." It surely was petrifying to hear the incessant whine of winds pockmarked by flying debris and falling trees, screams, cries for help, and unknown sounds that could mean nothing good during this fast-moving, violent storm.

**NOEL:** This November 2007 hurricane left 6,000 North Carolinians without power.

# O

**OCTOBER 18, 1906:** Yet another back-to-back hurricane for the Lowcountry! It first struck the four-masted schooner, the *Malcolm B. Seavey*, a 203-foot ship laden with 1,900 tons of phosphate rock. With shredded sails and four feet of water in the hold, the vessel eventually limped over the Charleston bar and into the harbor. Two schooners, the *Susan A. Bryan* and *Emma*, carried thousands of bushels of rice from Combahee River plantations. The storm blew the first ship all the way back to St. Catherines Island off Georgia; the second vanished, ship and crew never found. Otherwise, this hurricane was a much milder storm, though newfangled progress created some problems, such as downed electric wires setting trees on fire!

*Whipping wind and the rising water of storm surge is one of the biggest dangers in the Lowcountry.*

**OCTOBER 1910:** With only tropical storms along the Lowcountry for a couple of years, everyone on the Carolina coast was glad to at least see plenty of advance warnings for this storm. New and better alert systems kept boats in port and saved lives, as well as let citizens prepare for the onslaught. Although the storm stayed offshore, the storm surge was higher than any in decades. Tybee Island was evacuated, so fearful was everyone of a repeat deadly storm. It was a good thing since the sea covered the island and washed away many structures. So high and devastating was the water on the Combahee River in South

Carolina that it virtually put an end to the production of rice in the Lowcountry.

**OCTOBER 1947:** This storm seemed to have a nasty bent. Winds snapped an 84-foot pine tree that fell into a cabin, killing a 35-year-old man. A World War II veteran, who had just been acquitted in a fatal shooting, was hunting from a boat in the tidal creeks; his boat capsized and he drowned. A 14-year-old girl waded into water charged with 110 volts by a downed live wire; she managed to get out and ended up saving her grandparents' lives.

**OFFSHORE HURRICANE OF 1904:** A new century in the Lowcountry; the same old string of hurricanes. This storm caused the deaths of 11 African Americans from Charleston's beloved Mosquito Fleet. Even offshore, the 100-mile-per-hour winds managed to strip leaves off trees ashore; submerged rice fields; demolished corn and cotton crops; tore down barns and stables, crushing the animals within; leveled logging camps; stood tenant shacks on end; and otherwise was just a pest of a storm all the way up to Myrtle Beach and inland as far as Florence, South Carolina.

**OFFSHORE HURRICANE OF 1906:** Yet again, the U.S. Weather Bureau failed to provide any warning of this storm. "High combers struck the ship…and the wild wind shrieked amid the cordage" was how one ship captain described his introduction to the unexpected hurricane. Doors and hatches flew off the *Framfield*, a British steamship awash with 24,000 pounds of sugar, which clogged the pumps. Off the coast of South Carolina, the *Flora B. Rogers* and *J.W. Belano* were so damaged that the crews abandoned the ships. The *Job H. Jackson*, waterlogged at sea, also became a derelict. The bark *Ethel* was forced to be abandoned, some of its crew making it to shore at Myrtle Beach. *R. D. Bibber*, a schooner, found itself keel-up, crew scattered widely, many to drown. The many vessels, left in pieces afloat along a water corridor called "a menace to navigation," caused problems for years afterward. Ashore, this "offshore" hurricane's winds collapsed a church, killing an African American man still holding his Bible. After Pawley's Island was cut off from the mainland by storm surge, a young boy went back to rescue anyone left behind, saving an older man who had come along to help him but found himself stranded in shoulder-high water. In the piney woods of Plantersville, a tornado snapped off miles of pines midway, with damage exceeding $6 million in today's dollars and virtually wiping out the turpentine industry there.

**"ONCE IN EVERY TWENTY YEARS":** Early Lowcountry weather observers believed that major hurricanes only came about once every 20 years. By the end of September 1874, most folks were sure they had dodged that 20-year bullet. But no one told Mother Nature that rule, and so on September 28, a hurricane struck Tybee Island, Georgia. It washed away 50 feet of beach, leveled sand dunes, and basically drowned crops from Savannah to Charleston in saltwater. In Charleston, the bowsprit of a ship sliced a brick building in two, residents carted chickens into their homes to save them, and the weather service's storm flag blew away!

**OPEN BOAT:** Oddly, almost every hurricane seems to have some record of a person or family who unwisely elected to take refuge in a boat—often an open boat. While their decision is illogical, it could often become deadly, or at the minimum, fearful and miserable, as they tried to ride out the storm tossed hither and yon, or worse, slammed upon the shore. Even as recently as the 2016 hurricane *Matthew*, the *Island Packet* recorded the rather foolhardy attempt to ride out the storm on a shrimp trawler, which was eventually torn away from its mooring.

**OPHELIA:** In 2005, this hurricane drifted just offshore of the Outer Banks of North Carolina, yet still dropped more than 17 inches of rain and caused $70 million in damage.

## PALISADES OF FORT PINCKNEY:
A hurricane is nothing if not a cascade of catastrophes. You know what I mean: tree crashes into house, house falls on car, car falls on cat… or water breaches dunes, surges into diked land, destroys crops, overflows banks, backs up upstream, engorges ponds, engulfs roads, inundates all low-lying land. At the height of the 1804 hurricane, the entrance to Charleston Harbor must have seemed secure. However, the overpowering wind and water soon smashed the breastworks and palisades of Fort Pinckney, which allowed ships of all sizes to roar into the harbor. The downed fortifications knocked about boats, destroying the wharves. Tumbling wharves dumped goods into the sea. Many ships sank; others spilled into nearby marshes and onto land. A counting and scale house was tumbled

by the ship *Lydia*. Fifty tierces of rice were ruined when they filled with water. Cotton floated on the sea like white blossoms. It was said that slates blew from roofs and "flew in every direction like grapeshot." And yet, today, some folks think they can stay behind and "protect their homes and businesses"— it's never a good idea to believe you can out-muscle Mother Nature!

**PAWLEY'S ISLAND, SOUTH CAROLINA:** The 1916 hurricane was a whopper. On this island, thousands of trees blew down, many falling onto homes and businesses. The wind and water also destroyed bridges, cattle, horses and crops. There had been only an hour's warning when the captain of the *Ulana II* raced at great peril across Winyah Bay to Pawley's. Pounding on doors as he ran from summer cottage to summer cottage, he begged vacationers to evacuate. Several hundred people dashed through 100-mile-an-hour winds across the causeway to safety.

**PENN SCHOOL, ST. HELENA ISLAND:** For so long following a hurricane, there was no aid to be had other than neighbor helping neighbor. Then, the Red Cross began to offer some assistance. The ever-proud, self-reliant people of the Lowcountry often turned down offers of any kind of official aid, which seemed counter-productive, especially for the neediest citizens, usually the rural poor and African Americans. For example, after the devastating 1911 hurricane, Beaufort officials declined aid from the Red Cross, deeming it a "foreign, outside" agency they believed "ill advised" to invite into the Lowcountry. But blacks on the sea islands were truly destitute and with no resources for recovery. They went to the Penn School, which had been founded by northerners after the Civil War to help newly freed slaves. However, the school had been damaged by the storm.

**POOR LITTLE ELIZA:** The brig *Eliza* was the first casualty of a surprise hurricane in 1800. The September tropical weather was revving up, and this ship, filled with cotton bales, was completely disabled and had to be towed into port. By October 4, more than a dozen boats and a "valuable cargo of dry goods" were sunk off the South Carolina coast or in harbor. In the midst of the storm, a tornado struck at Cannonsburgh and a storm surge engulfed Sullivan's Island. A schooner, with all her "sails split to pieces," crashed onto shoals near Cape Romain. It was considered the most "tremendous and destructive" hurricane in the Lowcountry since 1783; but it would not be the last.

**PORGY AND BESS:** Hurricanes were the stuff literary types could make hay of. Charlestonian DuBose Heyward's novel *Porgy and Bess* (the basis of George Gershwin's opera of the same name) was an example. Catfish Row was the scene of a fearful night with Porgy and Bess huddled in their room praying for "the faint grey light…that told them that it was again day."

**QUESTION:** How deadly are storm surges?
Answer:
- 1900: Galveston, Texas: 8,000 deaths
- 1969: *Camille*: 24-foot storm tide in Mississippi
- 1989: *Hugo*: 20-foot storm surge in South Carolina
- 1992: *Iniki*: 6-foot storm tide on Kauai, Hawaii
- 2008: *Ike*: 20-foot storm tide in Texas

Just a few examples!

**RAINFALL:** Spiraling bands of rain from hurricanes can dump six, twelve, even twenty inches of water onto the land. While not generally as destructive as the storm surge, such massive rains can lead to flooding and spawn tornadoes or waterspouts.

**RESCUE:** The problem with not evacuating is that you may have to be rescued; this puts you and your rescuer (should one come) at great risk. The stories of rescue attempts are rampant, naturally; some are even successful. In one of my references, the index listing of the names of rescue vessels was only exceeded by the listing of ships damaged or lost at harbor, wharfside or offshore.

**RICE IS NICE:** ...unless it floats away. It was estimated that one stalled hurricane ruined 10,000 barrels of rice at Georgetown. Such disasters eventually put rice growers out of business.

**RIGHT FRONT QUADRANT:** This exceedingly dangerous part of a hurricane's spiral is a fist guaranteed to do great damage. The 1940 Lowcountry hurricane appeared after several years of relatively calm storms. In Georgia, Tybee Island took the first punch, with a barometric reading of 28.78 mm Hg, the lowest ever recorded in Savannah. One woman was cut so severely with flying glass that she bled to death. The town was a watery soup of flying bricks and falling oaks and sycamores. But it was South Carolina that got clobbered by the right front quadrant. It was the first hurricane to hit the South Carolina coast directly in 30 years, striking between Beaufort and Edisto Island. Hilton Head was said to have been "swept clean." Edisto's sand dunes, well anchored with palmetto trees, melted into the sea. Homes were washed away so thoroughly that the plumbing was all that was left of some. On the May River, Bluffton—in spite of its 20-foot bluffs—took a beating by "ocean height" waves. A 13-foot storm surge inundated St. Helena Island and Lady's Island; 33 blacks drowned. One young African American father took shelter in a tree with his newborn child, and they managed to survive. Practically all the shanties were washed away, as were creatures great and small. Folly Island was completely covered with water; the pavilion and pier were damaged and the merry-go-round and Ferris wheel vanished. On the Charleston wharf, the boats of the black fishermen—the Mosquito Fleet—were blown out of the water and onto railroad tracks and split wide open. Ballast stones were ripped from the Battery walkway. Fortunately, early warnings saved many lives, although the news, as usual, did not quite reach the hinterlands of the Lowcountry. To give some global perspective, this storm struck the U.S. just as 400 Nazi planes attacked England.

**RIP CURRENTS:** The strong winds of a hurricane can cause dangerous waves that break along the coast, producing rip currents, even at long distances away from the storm. These rip tides are channeled currents of water flowing away from shore, usually extending past the line of breaking waves. They can pull even strong swimmers away from shore. While you should swim parallel to the shore to get away from a rip current, the best bet is NOT to swim or surf at all when those red storm flags are flying!

## RISING SUN HURRICANE, 1700:

Summer has always been tenuous in the Lowcountry. Early colonists lamented "mosquitoes as big as dinner plates"; if there wasn't an epidemic of smallpox, there was one of yellow fever; and it was generally hot, muggy, and with the advance of a hurricane, just plain sweltering. On September 14, a storm plowed into the town and harbor of Charles Towne. An 80-ton brigantine was blown ashore and knocked down a gallows used to hang pirates. The *Rising Sun*, an 800-ton Scottish ship of 60 guns, had lost its masts in a Florida storm. As it sat offshore of Charles Town, awaiting retrofitting, the hurricane caused it to drag anchor and the ship was driven onto sandbars and foundered. The captain, crew and passengers, numbering around 100, all drowned. Washed ashore, the corpses were later buried and the island named Coffin Land (later renamed Folly Beach).

**R.J.:** This schooner and pilot boat was so battered offshore during the Lowcountry hurricane of 1811 that its captain was compelled to order the sinking ship abandoned. Scurrying into a 12-foot lifeboat, five men managed to bring aboard some water and bread. Hopes for immediate rescue were thwarted when a passing ship could not spot them in the erratic sea. When the storm abated, they rigged a sail and made headway toward a distant coastline, which they eventually reached after nine long, hard days at sea.

**ROSE-IN-BLOOM:** A beautiful name for a doomed ship, hey? At the height of the hurricane season, wealthy Lowcountry residents boarded this ship to sail to New York. The date was August 16, 1806. Like the later ill-fated *Titanic*, the passenger list included the rich and famous of the day. As the 49 passengers and crew prepared to sail on the beautiful late summer day, they were unaware of a storm brewing near the Bahamas. In the *Rose-in-Bloom's* wake, ships were caught up by the strengthening hurricane, all along the Georgia and Carolina coast. By August 22, the fierce storm caught up with ship. Soon enveloped in the furious hurricane, which was said to have frightened even the experienced mariners aboard, the captain fought to save the ship. Sails were shredded as the front, eye, then back end of the storm plowed over the ship. The *Rose-in-Bloom* was blown all the way to the New Jersey coast where it soon capsized. As water filled the ship, passengers and crew struggled to escape; many drowned in the attempt. The mostly Lowcountry survivors lashed themselves to the weather railing at the stern of the ship. Now, all but naked, cold, battered and terrified, they clung to the rail and one another; four more died. A hoped-for light turned out to be a star, not a rescue ship. The warmth of daybreak turned into a fearsome day of sunburn and salt-infested wounds. Rescued at last by a passing brig, the final tally was 23 of 49 passengers lost.

**"RUINOUSLY DRY":** A severe 1848 drought was ruining the Georgia cotton crop. A little rain seemed like a good thing until an October storm lashed the Florida and Georgia coast. Blowing with "unremitting violence," the storm then accosted the Carolinas. In 1851, a hot, dry summer abruptly changed into rafts of tin roofing and chimney bricks flying about in the rain squalls of a hurricane. By 1852, Lowcountry cotton and rice planter Thomas Chaplin, owner of Tombee, complained, "Rain. Rain. No cotton picked this week." But as a hurricane roared up the Florida and Georgia coast to the Carolinas, rain, rain and more rain ruined his crops for that year.

**SAFFIR-SIMPSON WIND SCALE:** Adopted by the National Hurricane Center in the 1970s, this scale provides a 1-5 rating of a storm's sustained wind speed. The goal is to estimate potential property damage.

**SANDY:** In late October 2012, this killer storm brushed the North Carolina coast with high winds and storm surge before heading northward to wreak havoc.

**SAVE YOURSELF:** I've read an endless list of the ways people tried to survive hurricanes. Just a few include: in a corn crib or outhouse, atop rafters, strapped to a sofa, tied to a beam, aboard a boat, in a house trailer, taking off a shirt or bloomers and tying tight to hold air as a makeshift life preserver, holding onto a tree with their teeth, and many more.

**SELLING THE SIZZLE?:** It's almost amusing how fast towns of the Lowcountry could put on their "Ya'll Come!" faces after a hurricane had barely passed. Residents often bragged how they had weathered a storm yet again, and after the 1911 hurricane, that the beach was even "better!" now that the storm had leveled the dunes. It was a natural response, since getting the tourist business back up and running was important. Indeed, reviving any industry still able to limp out of the wind and water and press on was important. Some people packed up and moved away, of course. But as we can easily see today, hurricanes seem to be no detriment to real estate booms. After all, it's all so lovely on a pretty summer's day!

**SEPTEMBER TORNADO:** On September 10, 1811, a tornado trumped the hurricane that spawned it. Said to have begun with a "rumbling noise," the twister zipped through downtown Charleston with "the rapidity of lightning." About 60-100 yards wide, the tornado touched down and destroyed much of Bay, Boundary, Church, Meeting, Tradd, King, Broad and Queen streets. Houses were leveled and roof tiles and slates spun through the air like weapons. Trees were uprooted; fences smashed. More than 20 lives were lost, and the financial toll reached more than $4 million.

**SHIPS IN DISTRESS-1:** While it's always petrifying to be at sea level and spy a hurricane headed your way, it's often difficult to imagine how terrifying it must have been to be at sea, in any size boat or ship, under such conditions. In August 1827, a hurricane pounded Florida, Georgia and South Carolina. The *Lavinia* was caught off-guard in a "tremendous cross-sea." Captains always quickly responded in hopes of saving their vessels: cut away the mizzenmast and topmast... work the pumps—but what do you do when the winds are literally ripping the ship apart? Twenty-five passengers aboard the *Brandt* watched all the ship's sails tear away in the storm, leaving the ship under "bare poles." The ship was awash in 60 feet of water, with waves breaking over it from every direction. A young cabin boy was washed overboard. Passengers manned the pumps for two exhausting days, but the hold was still filled with water. This was just two among a number of ships foundering on high seas in the claws of the hurricane. Some ships limped to port; others sunk. Some people lived; others died.

**SHIPS IN DISTRESS-II:** Here it comes again, yet another hurricane, August 1830. Yet another "war of the elements," as one man called it. As usual, the ships at sea were particularly vulnerable, caught off guard, when winds increased to hurricane force. Off the Georgia coast, the *New Prospect* all but lost a valuable cargo of rum, coffee and sugar before being rescued by the Wade, another ship also damaged in the storm. The *Empress* was headed to Charleston. Blown over on its larboard side, it lay with sails in the water for more than two hours, 60 passengers aboard, before it was righted. The schooner *Ranger* was wrecked near Bulls Island, South Carolina, and later found abandoned. Even tied securely to the wharf, ships were ruined and cargo lost: the *Atlantic* lost 200 pounds of sugar after the *Rasselas* smashed into the brig. The *Washington, Experiment, Carolatta, Othello, Pocahontas,* and many others were blown, bruised, capsized, bashed on shell banks, or otherwise destroyed on and off the Lowcountry coast. Don't leave out the *Maria, John Stoney, Exchange, Francis Ann, Comet, Frances Sophia,* and so many more, all at the mercy of the storm, all doomed.

**SHIPS OFFSHORE:** One of the most precarious positions one could find themselves in during an approaching or bearing-down hurricane was offshore the Lowcountry coastline. Captains and sailors found themselves at great risk of drowning. Accustomed to high winds and waves, the sudden change to hurricane force winds and water often caught ships by surprise. Sails and masts were ripped away like handkerchiefs and matchsticks; capsize often followed. Even attempts to keep a vessel afloat were made difficult when screamed orders could not be heard above the roaring wind. While some lives could be saved, drowning was often the outcome. If blown onto the bars of barrier islands or shifting shoals, ships were often shredded to smithereens. Some crippled vessels were lucky to limp back into port. In addition to lives, valuable cargo ranging from cocoa, sugar, indigo, rice, cotton, mahogany, naval stores, and more sunk to the ocean floor. Often, only a signature of random flotsam and jetsam was left to tell the story. Of course, following such devastation was a boon to ship chandlers, offering cordage, rigging, canvas and other repair articles and tools. Losses to a ship owner, whether he was a small-time fisherman or captain of a large vessel laden with imports or exports, were devastatingly substantial.

**SLOW-MOVERS:** Slow-moving hurricanes are the worst kind. When they stall, they can dump tons of water; if they saunter up the coast, they can blow and churn and otherwise cause more damage than if they pass quickly. In mid-July 1842, a slow-moving hurricane hit the Lowcountry. In early October, another slowpoke hurricane struck the Lowcountry coast. As it moseyed its way up the lower Georgia counties and beyond, the "heavy gale for 36 hours" just demolished trees, wharfs, buildings, riceland, and more. The storm surge was especially high. A third storm that year, at Halloween, ended this hateful, slow-moving trio of destruction-makers.

**SOLE SURVIVOR:** In the October 1811 hurricane, U.S. gunboat *No. 2* was trapped

*Hurricane Hugo takes out a car in Charleston*

in a turbulent sea off Cumberland Island, Georgia. In spite of trying every possible avenue to save the ship and stay afloat, the entire crew was drowned or pitched into the roaring sea. John Tier was lucky enough to grab a passing oar. For 29 hours, Tier clung to the oar until he was finally rescued by a passing ship. He was the only survivor of the 35 souls aboard the gunboat. It was his second time to survive a shipwreck that year!

**SPANISH REPULSE HURRICANE, 1686:** A perfect storm of heat, humidity and drought converged to create fertile ground for early Carolina colonists staring out at the Atlantic Ocean. With no warnings except, perhaps, a "mackerel sky" and "mare's tail" clouds, the few colonists, planters, traders, mariners and Native Americans went about their business as usual. Did anyone notice there had been the ominous "red sky at morn," by which sailors were said to be warned? Did keen observers notice the inland flocking of birds or the change in barometric pressure? Eventually hunkering down on the Charles Towne peninsula, the people suffered a great foreboding as the storm bore down on them, making landfall with the high tide. Destruction of the meager structures was inevitable; many people died. There was said to be "one scarce tree" left standing for miles around. While we cannot know the specific intensity of early hurricanes, this one was clearly a doozie. The only silver lining was that, due to the severity of the storm, the Spanish high-tailed it back to Florida. This hurricane was the first ever recorded in the Lowcountry, though many certainly preceded it. Despite a fear they would starve, the colonists remained.

**STORM SURGE:** The storm surge is not some sudden end-game event to a hurricane. It begins with the birth of the hurricane when spiraling winds raise a twisting column of water not only beneath the sea's surface, but also a dome several feet above the ocean. This column can be as much as 100 miles wide and moves with the hurricane as it advances. When the hurricane eventually approaches the shore, the dome of water is shoved upward, possibly as high as twenty feet. But this is only part of the surge. Huge waves can ride atop the dome and all this water, over and above the level of the sea at the time, creates an enormous destructive force.

**STORM TIDE:** The water level rise during a storm due to the combination of storm surge and the astronomical tide. For example, if a hurricane moves ashore at a high tide of 2 feet, a 15-foot surge would be added, creating a storm tide of 17 feet. High winds and storm tide topped with battering waves can be especially destructive.

**SUFFERING OF SAILORS-1:** Probably nothing is more frightening than to be awash or adrift at sea during an angry storm, no rescue in sight. In the August 1881 "fearful hurricane," 35,000 feet of lumber were sacrificed overboard in an attempt to save the *Brunswick*. The desperate sailors lashed themselves to the stump of the mizzenmast and yet were still bowled into the sea by the storm, then further assaulted by the blowing lumber. One 40-foot log smashed into one man's face "knocking all my front teeth down my throat." The others, who drifted away on a makeshift raft, eventually resorted to drinking seawater and "began to lose their minds." One man was said to have wanted to "eat his hands." They were finally rescued.

**SUFFERING OF SAILORS-II:** Also in August 1881, off the South Carolina coast, the *Mary G. Fisher*, a schooner carrying 210 tons of coal, encountered the hurricane. The captain was just 21 years old. First, the cross-seas washed away the lifeboat. Next, waves did enough structural damage to cause water to pour into the hold of the struggling ship. The rudder was torn off. Desperate crewmen climbed into the rigging for safety, but powerful waves upended the ship, which began to sink. One sailor swam to the surface, yanked off his clothes, and made his way over giant waves to a long piece of white pine. Over the next hours he was often knocked off the pole, but managed to grab back on. He finally caught up to a still-afloat piece of the cabin and clung to it. Often knocked off his perch by giant waves, he found himself surrounded by sharks. Cold, scared, and 25 miles offshore by now, he feared for his life. He called the sharks "not very pleasant companions" as he thought about his crewmates. So parched was the hallucinating sailor, that he thought he could "drink his own blood." For days and nights, alternately freezing, then baking to blisters in the hot sun, the man tried to survive. Incredibly, he was finally picked up off Bull's Bay and taken to a hospital in Savannah where he was treated and recovered from his hurricane ordeal.

**SULLIVAN'S ISLAND, SOUTH CAROLINA:** Edgar Allan Poe wrote *The Gold Bug* here. Even scarier was the 1804 hurricane that almost destroyed the entire island. Almost immediately upon the onslaught of the storm, 15-20 homes were washed out to sea. The only reason some homes were saved was that the sudden and violent storm blew and shoved sand dunes protectively around them.

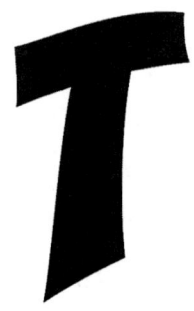

**TIMING:** Although "hurricane season" runs from June through November, most Lowcountry hurricanes strike during the months of August, September or October, when the ocean's temperatures are highest. Note that hurricanes can occur in other months, as well.

**TORNADOES:** It is well documented that hurricanes often spawn tornadoes. It is not exactly easy to spot a tornado in the midst of the furious onslaught of a hurricane. In an October 1797 hurricane, Allard Belin, master of Belmont Plantation near Georgetown, South Carolina, noted that he heard "a violent and destructive tornado pass… through"…ripping up trees by their roots and twisting off "the…tops of most others." In this dawn horror, the tornado picked up the house and kitchen house, "carried them nearly 100 yards" and tossed the buildings and inhabitants to the ground "with such violence that the structures were smashed to pieces, as were the bedsteads, tables, chairs, etc. in them." He further observed that the bodies of the overseer and "two very fine Negro boys…were… much mangled." In his own house, Belin heard a chimney collapse and his kitchen and washhouse "carried away." Stacks of harvested rice were blown into the river. A brief reprieve as the eye of the storm passed soon gave way to the winds "suddenly" returning and a storm surge that "came rolling up incredibly rapit" to "inundate the fields." In conclusion, this planter said it was "impossible…to paint the devastation and shocking spectacle of the whole plantation, now covered with ruins…"

**TROPICAL CYCLONE:** A rotating, organized system of clouds and thunderstorms that originates over tropical or subtropical waters and has a closed, low-level circulation. Tropical cyclones rotate counterclockwise in the northern hemisphere.

**TROPICAL DEPRESSION:** A tropical cyclone with maximum sustained winds of 38 miles per hour or less.

**TROPICAL STORM:** A tropical cyclone with maximum sustained winds of 39-73 miles per hour.

**TWIN HURRICANES:** In 1752, the Lowcountry was blasted by not one, but two hurricanes. In September, the second storm [see The Great Drougth Hurricane for the first] struck areas already made vulnerable by the earlier storm. At sea, 13 vessels were caught up in the high winds and seas. A two-masted, square-rigged scow was "beat to pieces" off St. Helena Island. Serious flooding occurred up and down the South Carolina and North Carolina coasts. The damage to the corn, peas and rice crops was so bad that exports were prohibited for a year because there was such fear that settlers might starve. Due to the great destruction of all fortifications at Charles Town, South Carolina, English merchants petitioned the king for protection for the "defenceless state" of the Georgia and South Carolina provinces.

**TYBEE TERROR:** In 1881, any advance warning of a forthcoming hurricane was still quite scant. The Savannah newspaper had reported about a storm in the Atlantic, but the U.S. Signal Corps did not issue any warning. So, residents and tourists went about their work and play in the August heat of Tybee Island, Georgia. Old salts were suspicious of the sudden heavy sea, and, sure enough, on Saturday, August 27, tourists found the mule-drawn streetcar service canceled due to heavy rain and high winds. The ongoing lack of warnings to outlying Lowcountry areas put people at risk. In addition to the washing away of the Tybee wharf, the hurricane battered strong homes as well as weak ones, with one of the most sturdy blown over into the ocean. Gas ignited and the house afloat burst into flames. One man broke his back and leg trying to rescue the residents, but most were crushed, and then burned, in the tragedy. Other homes were washed away or severely damaged. Trying to escape one home, everyone ran to another and found it in even worse condition. The storm surge of 12-14 feet above high tide pretty much kept erasing any available safe spot on the narrow island. Indeed, timbers and other debris from destroyed homes became projectiles difficult to avoid as people ran to escape. One woman described the live oaks and palmetto trees as "flying like straws" in the vicious wind. By the time the storm passed, a new inlet had been cut near the lighthouse and the beach was as "smooth as a billiard table." Bodies from nearby islands washed ashore at Tybee and many other islands. The final death toll was never known, but it included men, women, children, and entire slave families huddled in flimsy cabins swept to sea.

## UNDERSTANDING WARNINGS:

Hurricane Watch: Hurricane winds of 74 mph or more are possible; issued 48 hours ahead.

Tropical Storm Watch: Conditions of 39-73 mph winds are possible within 48 hours.

Hurricane Warning: Sustained winds of 74 mph or more are expected; 36 hours ahead.

Tropical Storm Warning: Winds of 39-73 mph are expected within 36 hours.

Extreme Wind Warning: Sustained winds of 115 mph or more are expected within an hour; take immediate shelter.

Tornado and flash flood watches and warnings are also possible. Do not ignore red storm flags on beaches, marine warnings, or any other warnings. Get a battery-operated weather radio in case power goes out. Have extra batteries on hand.

*Storm surge is responsible for most drownings in a hurricane.*

**VIDEO:** Instead of sticking around and seeing a hurricane up close and personal, settle for some great video; much safer! Excellent hurricane videos can be found on many websites—examples include National Geographic, CNN, The Weather Channel and YouTube. As I always say, "A video is worth a thousand words!"

**WARNINGS:** Early hurricane warnings included red flags with black centers, fire alarms sounding, the blowing of whistles, flashing signs, radio alerts or rockets fired into the air for ships at sea to hopefully spy. These were better than nothing. Today, of course, we have enough advance electronic and television warnings to create somewhat of a "Cry wolf" effect sometimes, but at least if we are prone to heed mandatory evacuations, we have a better chance to survive than did poor souls in earlier centuries.

**"WE SHOULD CERTAINLY HAVE A BLOW":** That was the opinion of seamen off the Georgia coast the day the 1928 hurricane struck. It had already raked Florida and now headed up a path close to what would be Interstate 95 today. As towns had progressed, there were new things to damage: large (and expensive) plate glass windows, gas service, electrical wires, telephone poles, streetcar service, apartment houses and snarled automobile traffic. Fifteen feet of sand washed off the beach at Folly Island, South Carolina. New crops of sweet potatoes and hay were destroyed at Georgetown. And hens blown into the marsh of the Ashley River were beaten with sticks and stuffed into sacks to be cooked and eaten later. Myrtle Beach, just getting its start as a resort, caught the end of the hurricane. New concerns included washed-out bridges, a new network to connect communities, and great erosion of beaches with homes built far too close to the shore.

**WHY YOU EVACUATE:** In 1804, a Georgetown, South Carolina, family of 15 was stranded on a small hill about 10-feet square after their home blew away. The water was so high that there was no land to be seen for a mile around. Fearing for their lives as the waves lapped their "island" perch, the family watched the tide recede enough for them to wade through chest-deep water to higher land, where they huddled, exposed to the storm for two more days!

**WILMA:** The outer bands of this October 2005 hurricane brought rain and wind all along the Outer Banks of North Carolina.

**WOMAN ON THE DECK:** Midday on August 27, 1911, a hurricane struck the *Bessie Whiting* off Sapelo Island, Georgia. Captain Lawry always sailed with his wife, Weona. The ship held 375,000 feet of yellow pine. As is typical, the captain ran before the storm for as long as possible, then close-reefed the sails. In spite of that, the jib boom and mainmast blew away, and the ship fell into a trough where heavy rains and enormous waves slammed the decks. The captain ordered the crew to lash themselves to the deckhouse. By that evening, the winds had increased to 130 miles per hour and the ship rolled and tumbled in the waves for 48 hours. On Tuesday morning, a vessel came near to rescue them. The exhausted crew bounded aboard, but Captain Lawry, his wife and a steward remained onboard. The *Bessie Whiting* drifted at sea for another day before a tugboat came near to offer food and drink, and a cutter towed the ship into harbor at Charleston. Those on shore watched with amazement at the romantic image of the woman with "a slender, girlish figure" in a "torn dress" with "long hair streamed out on the wind." As the viewers admired the incredible scene, Captain Lawry and the steward, with Weona standing between them, serenely smoked their pipes.

**WORLD WAR II HURRICANES:** Even near-hurricanes wreaked serious damage when coastal shipyards suffered setbacks during the war years. At the time, there were more resources like better warnings, and so a chance to move yourself and your boats or goods, etc., to safety or stronger shelter. The Coast Guard, military and police forces all played more of a role in the protection of life and property. Evacuations became more common. A new civil defense system was created to guard the coast and provide relief following a storm. And there was some hopeful science to try to put a damper on a hurricane. In the October 1947 hurricane, much of these new measures were put into practice. The storm was "seeded" to reduce its strength, which it did. Then much to the chagrin of scientists, the hurricane "rejuvenated," did an about-face, and headed straight for the Georgia-South Carolina coast! Advisories were issued, storm flags went up, and mandatory evacuations were put into place. Sirens screamed, along with the winds, as the storm plunged ashore. In addition to the usual damage, C-47 transport planes at Hunter and Chatham airfields were damaged and hangars destroyed.

**"WRITTEN ON THE STORM":** The October 7, 1783 hurricane inspired this recounting by an eyewitness and poet:

*In strict obedience to the Heav'nly power*
*At early dawn the clouds began to lour;*
*All nature seems to wear a gloomy face,*
*Destruction now approaches every place;*
*Rough Aeolus his quarter thus had chose,*

And from his north-east seat in anger blows;
Whilst Neptune mounts his fatal, wat'ry car,
And quick dispatches Triton from a-far;
High on the seas, the Trident-bearer soars,
And bends his way to shew his power with all his might;
Whilst rains most rapidly in torrents fall,
And num'rous ills present themselves to all.
How shall I paint the sad, distressful day,
And tell how supportively the seas did play?
Alas! 'tis horrid for myself to think,
Of vessels that I saw begin to sink:
One at a wharf, careening as she lay
Became a sad remembrance of the day!
Others, at anchor, met an equal doom;
And for succeeding wrecks, as quick made room.
A schooner next, when mooring near the shore
Did, with her bowsprit, spur a little store;
Sorry and fear appears in ev'ry face,
She carries now the house quite out of place.
I saw soon after that, eye witness me,

## 162

*Three smaller vessels found'ring in the sea,*
*'Twas by a wharf, where fish have oft been spar'd*
*And fishermen in losses too have shar'd.*
*But oh! How sad and lamentably great,*
*Must be the tales that others will relate!*
*May Heav'n ordain, that this has only been,*
*The real loss which we ourselves have seen.*

**X MARKS THE SPOT!:** Hurricanes are rather notorious for unburying buried treasure. Obviously, hurricanes often sink treasure ships, but such storms also scour beaches and unearth coins, rings, ancient Native American artifacts and other valuables. Remember Mel Fisher? In 1885, he found $500 million in treasure (doubloons, pieces-of-eight, cannons, emeralds, and much more) in less than 100 feet of water, where the treasure had lain from the hurricane-induced shipwreck of the Spanish galleon *Atocha*. Until Florida could decide if it was "finder's keepers" or not, the treasure was "arrested" and kept in a Key West jail for safety. Fisher prevailed.

**"YELLOW FEVER, TOO!":** Savannah suffered a double whammy during the catastrophic hurricane of 1854. The city was trying to cope with a major yellow fever epidemic when the storm hit. The hurricane was so powerful that the employees of the *Savannah Republican* were afraid to venture from the building where they were trying to get the paper out. One editor's vivid recounting of the storm was later reprinted in the *New York Daily Times*. Savannah's streets were so littered with trees that they were impassable, even on foot. The many beautiful squares were damaged, and roofs torn off many buildings downtown. Even gaslight posts were blown over. Saltwater surged into the waterworks, ruining the city's water supply. Two lighthouses were toppled. Fields looked like "an angry ocean," said one observer. Up the coast, Bluffton, Beaufort, Port Royal and Edisto were especially battered. Charleston, too, was suffering from a yellow fever epidemic. By the time the storm vacated the Lowcountry, well more than a thousand people had died from the disease, not counting the toll as a result of this particularly horrendous hurricane.

**YOU KNOW...:** You know the water was too high for too long, when after a hurricane, the bodies of turtles and fish litter the land!

*Most states have very specific evacuation routes. If you wish to go another way, you'd better plan to evacuate early!*

**ZONES:** The South Carolina Emergency Management Department has a website where you can learn which hurricane evacuation zone you are in. This site helps you determine your evacuation route and vulnerability to storm surge. All of this information will help you prepare better for the "next one." Go to www.scemd.org.

# BIBLIOGRAPHY

## The Great Deluge
Douglas Brinkley

Although not about the Lowcountry, obviously, this tome on *Katrina* by this incredible historian who lived through that Category Five storm, is an educational and emotional rollercoaster ride through all things hurricane. A worthy read.

## Hurricane Destruction in South Carolina: Hell and High Water
Tom Rubillo

Covers 30 major hurricanes that have hit South Carolina since the 1800s.

## Islands, Capes, and Sounds: The NC Coast
Thomas J. Schoenbaum

Excellent book with lots of great info and photos on that spectrum of the Lowcountry. The

Lowcountry shares a unique coastal neighborhood with our friends to the north and south.

**LOWCOUNTRY HURRICANES:**
**Three Centuries of Storms at Sea and Ashore**
Walter J. Fraser Jr.

Copyright 2006, this outstanding recounting of the insanity of incessant hurricanes in the Lowcountry is missing more current storms, but is a wonderful, well-researched, history-rich read. Includes black and white photos.

**North Carolina's Hurricane History**
Jay Barnes

Lots of great photographs and information.

**The Outer Banks of North Carolina**
David Stick
The University of North Carolina Press

Fascinating book on all things Outer Banks.

History back to the start of America, all those Cape Hatteras shipwrecks, hurricanes and more.

### South Carolina's Lowcountry
Anthony Chibbaro

One of those amazing Images of America books, this one features many historical photographs of the Lowcountry and will help you visualize this lovely land in the past.

### Tales of the Barrier Islands of Beaufort County, SC
Pierre McGowan

Renowned as the "Gullah mailman," Pierre's book is not really about hurricanes, it gives you a great look at life in the Lowcountry before there was so much of the current development. An enjoyable read, especially if you wish you'd grown up as a kid and a teen on these beautiful waterways.

## Tombee, Portrait of a Cotton Planter

This outstanding and extensive diary of Thomas Chaplin, with a compelling introduction by Theodore Rosengarten, will help you see just how hard plantation life was for masters and slaves alike. Described as "unrelenting misery," all had to work together to survive the Lowcountry heat, disease, planting and harvest seasons, and hurricanes. This is a big, discouraging read, but worth it. At times, you can actually tour Tombee, now a private home, on St. Helena Island. It was saved from destruction by Jim Williams, of *Midnight in the Garden of Good and Evil* fame.

## The World of the Salt Marsh:
## Appreciating and Protecting the Tidal Marshes of the Southeastern Atlantic Coast
Charles Seabrook

The book to read if you live or own property in the Lowcountry. It helps to understand the machinations of the salt marsh and the many threats to its ecological survival. This book will make you see the coast and the wetlands in a different way and care a lot more about your role in their protection and survival.

## HURRICANE QUOTATIONS

"At the end of August and the beginning of September…travelers on the water here are full of fear of the great storm winds which are called hurricanes in the English language and have been described to be the most terrifying."—German pastor and immigrant to Georgia

"How good ye Great God has Been to me, in keeping my Sperits up, and sending me Safe to Shore, after having nothing but Death before my Eyes, for Severall hours."—Artemas Elliot, Hurricane of 1752, Charles Towne.

Following the twin hurricanes of 1752, Peter Manigault was consumed, he said, with "Pity upon the poor unfortunate Condition of the Sufferers in Carolina."

Anyone found "*picking up, purloining and plundering, the Goods, Wares, Household Furniture, Sails, Mast, Rigging and other Things carried away by the Violence of the Wind and Waves*" after the 1752 hurricane were warned they'd be prosecuted. Slaves and Negroes would be sent to the work house and punished.

The hurricane...shut down completely on the ship and the men on it. Drunkenly buffeted, half-drowned, hardly able to see, unable to hear, each in the strangeness and terror was alone. The dark green, wind-carved, rain-pitted swells had turned black, had swollen, fretted and tumbling with white sheets...that made the speed of the wind visible in the lightning blasts of foam." — *On the slave ship Africa, 1752; History of South Carolina.*

Advice to those new in the Lowcountry provinces from Henry Laurens: *"About the middle of August begin to be much upon your Guard about tempestuous Weather. I caution you because you have never seen a Hurricane, you shd have Bars of strong Wood ready to fasten in all your Windows, keep every Article liable to Damage six Inches off your Floors, and nothing so low as the common Surface of the Earth in the Cellars, these you must expect to brim full, your Houses and Outhouses over-*

flowed your fences blown down...prepare against the worst while The Weather is fair. Save all those Cypress Boards...for repairing Fences and in case of Disaster send for [the slaves.]"

*Black and white all mixed together*
*Inconstant, strange, unhealthful weather*
*Burning heat and chilling cold*
*Dangerous to both young and old*
*Boisterous winds and heavy rains*
*Fevers and rheumatic pains*
*Houses built on barren land*
*No lamps or lights, but streets of sand*
*Everything at a high price*
*But rum, hominy, and rice.*
—Captain Martin

Lieutenant Archer, British naval officer, HMS Phoenix, 1780, off Savannah, Georgia: "At eight in the morning I came up...found it blowing hard from the east-northeast with close-reefed topsails upon the ship, and heavy squalls at time....At twelve, the gale still increasing....In the evening...secured all the sails; Squared the booms; saw the boats *all made fast; new lashed the guns; saw the carpenters had the tarpaulins and battens all ready for the hatchways; got the top gallant mast down; jib boom and spirit sail...fore and aft.... The poor devils of birds...came over the ship and dashed themselves down upon the deck....At eight o'clock a hurricane....The purser frightened out of his wits....The two marine-officers as white as sheets....the poor ship...shaking her sides, and groaning....Sir Hyde upon deck lashed to windward! I soon lashed myself alongside of him.... 'Shall we cut the mainmast away?' 'Ay! Fast as you can...' I went into the chains with a pole-axe, to cut away the lanyards; when a very violent sea broke right on board of us, carried everything upon deck away, filled the ship with water, the main and mizzen-masts went....the ship thump and grinding under our feet....unmerciful sea lifted and beat us up...high among the rocks."*

Alas! What must be the feelings of them
Whose barks had to yield to the storm! The
Loud winds, mingled with darkness above,
Whistling over the foaming wave,

*And nothing beneath save the fathomless Deep—how must the seaman have felt when He grasped for a hold, and the flying spume Passed between his fingers! And how doleful His cry when "heard along the deep!"*
—*Savannah Republican* editor and poet on the 1815 hurricane

"All was desolation....Every field, every plantation shows marks of ruin...nothing but wild fennel, bushes,...briars to be seen."—The Reverend Archibald Simpson, Beaufort, South Carolina, 1780

"You might as well be philosophical about hurricanes—there's nothing else you can do about them."—1908 hurricane survivor

*The rain fell in tub fulls, and beat down the corn,
Pea, pumkin and tatoe vines matted were borne,
Like cobwebs in autumn, while sapling and tree
Were popping and nodding like waves on the sea.* —Poem on the 1817 hurricane